enCouraged

Kathy DiSarli and Valerie Crawford

WestBow
PRESS
A DIVISION OF THOMAS NELSON

WestBow Press books may be ordered through booksellers or by contacting:

WestBow Press
A Division of Thomas Nelson
1663 Liberty Drive
Bloomington, IN 47403
www.westbowpress.com
1-(866) 928-1240

Because of the dynamic nature of the Internet, any web addresses or links contained in this book may have changed since publication and may no longer be valid. The views expressed in this work are solely those of the author and do not necessarily reflect the views of the publisher, and the publisher hereby disclaims any responsibility for them.

Any people depicted in stock imagery provided by Thinkstock are models, and such images are being used for illustrative purposes only.

Certain stock imagery © Thinkstock.

ISBN: 978-1-4497-4384-0 (sc)

Library of Congress Control Number: 2012905142

Printed in the United States of America

WestBow Press rev. date: 04/26/2012

TABLE OF CONTENTS

*name changed to protect privacy

PREFACE

Can we talk?

Why are those three words so very frightening to hear . . . and sometimes to say?

That's how this all began. God said, "Can we talk?" Actually it was more like, "I'm talking to you. You need to listen." Little did we know He was talking to other women and preparing them to join us in this crazy journey, as He prompted us to ask them, "Can we talk?"

God has been amazing, persistent and more than a little patient as we have ignored Him, fought with Him, negotiated with Him and finally obeyed Him. Why is it so tough to tell our own story? God has been so very good, yet opening our mouths seems to take a crowbar sometimes. As much as we denied His calling to tell His story of our lives, we are now thrilled to be writing an actual introduction to an actual book . . . . years later!

From the birth of an idea to gathering writers to editing and publishing, God has led us each step of the way, showing us the people He wanted to use and giving us the words He wants to share with you.

God has blessed each of these writers by bringing them into a closer fellowship with Himself and we pray that through reading their stories and by delving into His word, you may enter into a deeper fellowship with Christ as well.

We invite you to walk along with us through some of our lives' most sacred moments. So, grab your tissues, your Bible and your pencils and be prepared to laugh, to cry and be challenged. Be ready to experience Jesus enCouraging you just as thoroughly as He has enCouraged all of us.

Kathy Di Sarli & Valerie Crawford

We proclaim to you what we have seen and heard, so that you also may have fellowship with us. And our fellowship is with the Father and with His Son, Jesus Christ. We write this to make our joy complete.

1 John 1:3-4

ACKNOWLEDGEMENTS

We would first and foremost like to thank our Lord and Savior Jesus Christ, without whom none of us would have a story to tell.

We would also like to give our most heartfelt thanks to you:

Our wonderful, IT savvy, patient husbands who prayed with us, listened to us and gave us time to work on this project.

The amazing women who have allowed us the privilege of holding their precious stories and sharing them with the world. What courage you all display!

The dedicated prayer team that has kept this book covered in prayer from the early stages of rough drafts through production.

The early review groups that worked through this study with us allowing us to edit and refine the content.

Our home churches and their leaders for their support and encouraging words during this process.

What an adventure this has been. You have enCOURAGEd us more than you will ever know! We thank you all!

PIGPENS AREN'T JUST FOR PRODIGAL SONS!

Red . . . White . . . Blue . . . One after the other the undercover cars started racing into our driveway. I knew I was in trouble. Our living room was suddenly full of FBI agents and other law enforcement officials. All I could do was sit terrified with my mother on our couch. They searched our home for guns and gang paraphernalia, and then showed us pictures of a 16 year old boy who'd been beaten to death . . . . by what they said was an order given by my boyfriend. You'd think that experience would be enough to scare me out of the worst choices I'd ever made, but instead, I was about to get deeper into trouble than I'd ever been before. And every bit of it was my fault.

I never dreamed I would be faced with a day like that in my life. After all, I'd accepted Christ at a very young age, and there has never been any doubt that I'd been saved, that I belonged to Jesus, and that I should be living for God. So what happened? What went wrong? How did I end up here in a house full of law enforcement agents facing such horrific events? Maybe it all started when I was a child so let's start there.

Most of my elementary years were spent in a Christian school surrounded by Christian influences. My parents made sure I was in church every time the doors were open, so it was no surprise that I made a decision very early on to invite Christ into my heart as Lord and Savior. I was immersed in scripture and Bible study and my knowledge of God began to grow. What I neglected to learn, however, was how to have and how to grow into a one on one relationship with our Savior. Through a warped knowledge, I began to see Him as a God only capable of wrath. I grasped on to the legalistic beliefs that surrounded me and ignored the grace and love He has for each of us. I literally pictured God as a referee who was sitting up high watching my life like some kind of sporting event, ready to throw a penalty flag whenever I messed up. I thought Him to be a God who would punish in order to prove His power and, unfortunately as I grew in age, that misunderstanding of who God is never changed. I got older but my faith remained quite infantile.

As time progressed I soon would be faced with the challenges all teenagers face. I, like many, soon began making decisions that I knew were against what I had been taught to believe. But I was done living in fear of wrath, I was determined to find out why all the kids around me weren't being destroyed with the worst possible plagues and strokes of random lightening. Well, one compromise led to another and before long I wasn't even considering what God was thinking of me. I was only worried about what my peers were thinking of me.

By my last year in High School I had managed to separate myself from my Christian friends, and my new friends, well let's just say they could only wear certain colors because of their loyalty to their gang nation. That's right, good little girl from the suburbs now sneaking around and associating with known gang members. Satan can find you anywhere; it doesn't matter where your neighborhood or church membership is located. Sin doesn't care what area of town you live in or what your economic status is. That kind of false sense of security can be mighty dangerous. Our children are not safe from Satan's lies and attacks just because they make professions of faith. If anything the target on them is enlarged and Satan will try to do all he can to destroy not only our children and us, but the reputation of Christ as well. Saved in the eternal realm indeed we are, but safe here on earth from Satan's tricks we are not. We must give our children all the weapons needed to fight the enemy and teach them how to use them. We must make them aware of the enemy, not just shield them from the fact there IS an Enemy out there. Scary, I know but undoubtedly the Enemy will at some point come for us and our children and if they are unaware of the Enemy's presence, how on earth can we expect them to escape being captured? Genesis 4:7b *But if you do not do what is right, sin is crouching at your door; it desires to have you, but you must master it.*

I was not ready when the Enemy came for me. I was still so naive about the danger I was putting myself in by being around all the violence. The first time I remember being scared was at a party where we (my friends and I) were apparently not wanted. I of course was so busy trying to be cool and fit in that I didn't really notice what was going on all around me. Suddenly, I was grabbed by a guy I did not know. At this moment I was still unclear what was happening. I thought maybe this was horseplay or a joke of some kind. That is until I saw the sawed off shot-gun in his other hand. Things began moving in slow motion. I couldn't believe it. This guy was threatening to kill me if we didn't all leave. It's fair to say that by this time most of the people I had come to the party with were already running back to their cars (so much for watching out for me). Thankfully a few of them did stay behind and after convincing this guy that we would leave without a fight and not come back in any kind of retaliation, he let me go. I remember my legs felt like they had weights on them as I ran back to the car. I wondered the entire time if I was going to get shot as I ran. Talk about a wake—up call, but even that was not enough to scare me away from this new exciting lifestyle I was so determined to live. By this time I did know that the way I was living was not right in many areas, I just hadn't realized how far away from Right I had really gotten. As I was distancing myself from God I was gaining a hatred for myself that I didn't even realize I was doing. I thought I was being tough but really I was just shutting down so I wouldn't feel anything, especially the Holy Spirit trying to guide me back. I disassociated myself with anyone who was a reminder to me of God, church, or any of those things you don't want to be convicted of when you are in the midst of pleasing yourself rather than God. I enjoyed the fact that I was being noticed. It didn't matter to me that it wasn't positive attention. I just liked the fact that I wasn't blending in with the background anymore. Basically, I compromised myself and my beliefs in order to be accepted. It's amazing what excuses we can come up with to rationalize something we know is wrong into being acceptable. Whether it is as simple as a TV show we know is not pleasing to God ("but everyone else in the church watches it too") or a lifestyle that is socially acceptable but clearly biblically unacceptable, we humans are experts at rationalizing our behavior. *Romans 12:2 "Don't conform any longer to the pattern of this world, but be transformed by the renewing of your mind.*

Well as you know, one bad choice usually leads to another and another and . . . you get the drift. Along with that drift came "the guy." You know what I mean when I say "the guy." We all remember that one guy you want to notice you so badly. That guy who seems to be in a whole different league but still you want him for yourself. Well lucky for me he did notice me. I say that in complete sarcasm because the day I met him is the day any "luck" I had went right out the door. But I couldn't resist. He was one of those guys who was the center of attention no matter where he was and whatever room he was in was the room everyone else wanted to be in. atural born leader, and leader he was. He was a leader of a gang out of Las Vegas and he was now increasing his territory. Our lives crossed at a mutual friend's house where I fell head over heels immediately. He kept his "business" away from me for the most part. I mean I was privy to some things but it wasn't until the FBI showed up to take him away one afternoon that I realized how deep into things I had really gotten. When I say the FBI showed up I mean they really showed up and they brought their state and local friends with them as well. They came in with guns pulled ready to do whatever they had to do in order to take this guy down. After he was apprehended and gone they proceeded to tell me what all he was being charged with, which to save this story from being 20 pages long we will just say that it was pretty much every criminal act I had ever heard of. But instead of being horrified, I sat there and defended him like he was some kind of hero. I know there are women out there reading this who can relate to that. We sit and watch those Lifetime movies and yell at the girls to wise up and move on and yet we protect the man (because we love him and we can change him) from whom we need protection most of all.

While you would think this relationship would find its separation papers due to the obvious factor of incarceration, the exact opposite happened. I became consumed with doing whatever I could to help my boyfriend during his time of need. He would call me his queen and I would do whatever he asked.

And then there was that Saturday, when our home was suddenly filled with all kinds of different law enforcement agents. After the exhausting questioning, accusing, and heartbreaking stories told by the law enforcement agents was over, I again began to do what I did best, which was defend this guy and nothing in my life changed. If anything my heart grew harder and I began to feel even more alone and felt as if happiness was only going to be able to be found in the love I had for this guy.

My life wasn't my life anymore at all. I had forgotten what I liked to do and what made me happy, and all my time and thoughts were consumed with what made him happy. If he had a good day then I had a good day. If he had a bad day then I had a bad day. I was spiraling down into a pit of despair and depression and one day decided I had had enough and I was going to end it. Not end it with him but end my life. I made a pitiful attempt at suicide, landing myself in the hospital briefly, but I was actually released and back home that evening.

I still couldn't see how much of my life I was wasting by looking for acceptance in this guy. God must have been looking down at me with His arms held out crying . . . "Kathy can't you see you have already found acceptance in me? Come back." But I had turned so far from God that I couldn't hear what He was saying to me. I know many of you reading this right now know exactly what it feels like to be turned that far away from God. For me it was immersing myself in this lifestyle full of unhealthy relationships and friendships that brought about all kinds of sinful acts. For others it could be pornography, an addiction that you just keep coming back to, an abortion you are trying to run away from, or even a relationship that has gone too far outside of marriage. It can be different for all of us, but if we continue down a path of disobedience to God eventually we will not be able to hear Him anymore. *(Isaiah 59:2 But your iniquities have separated you from your God; your sins have hidden his face from you, so that he will not hear.)* And that is where I was in my life. I couldn't hear God and I wasn't talking to God. And that just opened the door even wider for Satan to come in and wreak havoc on my life.

Eventually I moved to be closer to this guy. I lived in a one bedroom apartment on a bad side of town. I used to sleep with a fan on to help drown out the sounds of people running past the windows and the sirens from police cars that went by several times a night. While living there I got involved in making drug transactions for my boyfriend. I would go to very dangerous areas by myself and buy drugs and then I would hide them on my body and transport them into the jails for him. This was quite an obstacle considering the pat down you have to go through before being allowed into the visitation areas of the jail. This along with other things I allowed my body to be used for, some of which are even now too difficult to share with you, were the most humiliating things I have ever been a part of. I allowed my body to be used in humiliating ways just to be able to continue to be with this guy. This guy had me from the beginning. I defended him. I put myself in dangerous places for him. I even broke the law for him. (Can you imagine if I put that kind of loyalty and devotion into my relationship with Christ what all could be accomplished for His kingdom? Imagine what we all could get done for Him if we really made Him, our God, the one we serve instead of other people. *Luke16:13 No servant can serve two masters. Either he will hate the one and love the other or he will be devoted to one and despise the other.* So far in my story who would you say my master seemed to be? God or my boyfriend? Who would people say your master is? God or someone else?)

So how did things change? What happened to make me see the errors of my ways and come to my senses? It had to be something huge, right? It wasn't a huge event at all. God had tried the huge events and I just ignored them so He went with a more subtle approach. I woke up one morning in this crummy little apartment and watched as this huge cockroach crawled across the floor. Roaches weren't uncommon in this apartment at all. In fact there were a lot more of them than there were of us. But for some reason this roach got me to thinking. Thinking about my life and what kind of life I wanted to have and even what kind of life I might want to have for any future children. This wasn't it at all. So after struggling with the decision to leave, I finally packed my car with what would fit in it and left. I didn't tell anyone I was leaving because I knew that I could and would be talked into staying. So, I just left. Sounds so simple doesn't it? If you have ever tried to "just leave" or are in the middle of trying to leave now you know there is nothing simple about it at all.

So that was it, a roach. I like to call it my "holy roach," an angel sent down in roach form to get me to thinking about what I really did and did not want out of life. I can honestly say I never thought I would be thanking God for those roaches in that apartment, but you never know what God is going to use to change your life. In fact, you may be what He is going to use to change someone else's life. If He can use a roach, He can definitely use one of us.

There were so many people that never gave up on me through this journey. My parents never gave up even though I know they must have been so frustrated after years and years of praying and not seeing any change. The church I attended at the time prayed continuously for me for years. When I think of these people and their faithfulness I think of *James 5:16 "The prayers of a righteous man are powerful and effective."* And I believe it is because of these prayers that I was kept safe for as long as I was and brought back home.

So now what? I wish I could say that after returning home I began living a life more pleasing to God, but I didn't. I began again putting myself in different but still wrong situations. The alcohol, the drugs, the sinful relationships . . . . probably the lowest point was when I realized I had used cocaine everyday for two weeks, was looking to buy more and scared I wouldn't find any.

My life was a crazy mess and still God wanted to work in it. During this time is when I met my husband. I didn't see that as being God at work at the time but it definitely was. About 6 months into the marriage we found out we were pregnant. We were so excited! I could just picture our new family and things in my life seemed to be falling into place. We decided my husband should re-enlist in the Air Force so that we would be able to better provide for this family we were about to have. Then the day came when we found out our baby was gone. Just like that all of our excitement was gone. I got mad. Mostly I got mad at God. Could this be my punishment for all the things I had done wrong in my life? That's what I thought. Notice I didn't include God into my equation until something went wrong and then I blamed Him. My husband on the other hand, turned to God for comfort and accepted Christ as his personal Savior.

As anyone who has ever dealt with grief knows, life doesn't stop and wait on you to grieve, it keeps moving on and for us that meant we were moving to our first assignment . . . . Small Town, GA.

So let's catch up. Newly married, just lost a baby, moved away from all that I was comfortable with, family, friends, etc . . . And for what? I felt like I had been abandoned. I was lonely and so unsatisfied with my life. This is not what I had signed up for! But God hadn't abandoned me at all. *(Hebrews 13:5 "Never will I leave you: never will I forsake you.)* He knew that in order to get me to realize my need for Him, He had to remove all the things that were causing me distractions.

Our first apartment there in Georgia was about a half mile down the road from a beautiful church. Shortly after moving in we began visiting the church. Let me assure you that even though things might have looked ok on the outside, inside I was still a mess. I was still hurt and angry and truthfully the only reason I was in church is because it meant so much to my husband. Am I ever thankful for my husband and his fire for Christ. Sunday after Sunday we would sit in the balcony of the church and listen. I can't tell you how many times I left the church on Sunday afternoon feeling like the message was being directed straight at me. I remember reading a scripture in Romans 7:15-19 where Paul talks about the struggle of the flesh. It says *"For what I want to do I do not do, but what I hate I do . . . For I have the desire to do what is good, but I cannot carry it out. For what I do is not the good I want to do; no, the evil I do not want to do-this I keep on doing."* This was how I felt. I didn't want to desire fleshly things any more, but I did. I didn't want to be angry any more, but I was. I wanted to do what was right and good, but when it came time to make a choice I still always seemed to make the wrong one. So I began praying that God would change the desires of my heart. I continually prayed that prayer and though I still made wrong choices sometimes . . . and still do . . . I began being convicted of them. If you're a Christian you know that being under conviction is not the best feeling in the world. But I was so excited about it, because it meant that my heart hadn't grown so cold that I couldn't feel God anymore. Maybe I still had a chance at this whole Christian thing. *John 10:28 "I give them eternal life, and they shall never perish; no one can snatch them out of my hand."* That means I am still in His hand. He never let me go.

Could it actually be that God wasn't like a referee, but like the Father I had heard Him referred to as? And if He is our Father then just like my earthly father forgave me and accepted me in his home, then maybe God would still accept me too. Most everyone knows the story of the prodigal son. If not you can find the story in Luke 15:11-31, but it goes something like this. The son leaves his father's home to find a life of fun and freedom and soon finds himself lonely, dirty, in the middle of a pigpen, and yearning to be back home. But would his father accept him back? After all he left by his own choice. Well if you know the story you know the ending. If you don't know the story I am about to ruin the ending for you. The father saw him from a long distance and accepted him with open arms. Not only accepted him but threw a party for him and rejoiced in his homecoming . . . . This is my life. There I was, feeling so lonely and dirty and hurt by all the wrong things I had done in my life, and there God was with His arms stretched wide to welcome me back in. Not just let me back in but He forgave me of all those sins I had committed and set them apart from me. AMAZING!!!! *"Amazing Grace how sweet the sound that saved a wretch like me!"* Truly God's grace is always Amazing and always abundant!

So maybe the question at the beginning of my story about what happened? What went wrong? Isn't the question that God wants me to answer. I think maybe He wants me to find out what went right. See we all undoubtedly, Christian or not, will be faced with choices that if made wrong can land us right smack in the middle of a pigpen eating the slop the pigs around us eat. But we don't have to stay there.

God at an early age allowed me the opportunity to learn His word. Scripture is so powerful and there were many times after I finally came to the realization that my life had to change that scripture from my childhood would just pop in my head and I could hear and feel God communicating with me, telling me not to give up and to keep moving forward in Him. *Luke 4:12 "For the word of God is living and active."* So even at an early age that was something that went right. It's never too late to open your Bible and let the power of God's word speak to you.

The power of prayer that surrounded me was also what went right. When I was too lost to see I needed prayer, God still honored the prayers of others who daily lifted me up to Him and interceded on my behalf. Don't ever underestimate the power of prayer. Probably the most pivotal point in my life was when I began to pray that the desires of my heart be changed. If you're in need of a changed heart, pray for it. Don't give up on that someone you have been praying for, for what seems like years. God's timing is not our timing but He does hear our prayers.

Going to church even though it wasn't because I wanted to at first was also something that went right. Even though my main motivation for going back to church was to please my husband, God used that setting and His words spoken through that preacher to penetrate my heart so deeply that I would many times leave in tears. So if you are looking for a starting place to get your life back on track, go to church. Yes it may be uncomfortable and yes you may feel out of place but if you go to a God loving, Bible preaching church sooner or later the messages are going to hit home. And you may find yourself, like me, excited for the first time in a long time, convicted and convinced that your life has to change.

Don't let me mislead you. Though life with Christ is wonderful, I still face difficult trials and temptations. The strongest temptation for me is to allow the guilt I feel about all the times I have failed make me feel worthless and unusable by God. See once Satan realizes you won't fall for a certain temptation anymore, he moves to trying to make you feel guilty over all the times you fell for it in the past. I have passed up opportunities to witness to some of the people that have been brought into my life because I allowed Satan to convince me that I had no right to talk to them about God. After all I was just as guilty as they were. The difference is that I have confessed those sins to Christ and have been forgiven of those sins. By not sharing what Christ has done for me through grace and forgiveness I am keeping that grace to myself. And keeping that grace to myself, not allowing people to see what God has done in my life gives Satan yet another victory.

If I could go back and change things I definitely would. But what is so amazing to me now is watching God take this part of my life that was far from pleasing to Him and turning it into something good. *Romans 8:28 All things work together for good of them that love God and are called according to His purpose.* God is very able to take the worst of ourselves and still work it to His good (and ours) if we just give it over to Him and allow Him to. That's why I am sharing this now. It's not because the details of my life are important. It's because God wants me to share the grace He has so abundantly poured out on me with all of you.

If you are in a lifestyle now that is wrong, get out. God may have you reading this book just to hear that message. God promises us in 1 Corinthians 10:13 that when we are tempted He will provide us a way out. So if you are in a pigpen right now, find the way out. Don't focus on the wrongs of your life. Look forward to a future and thank God for being what went Right in your life. My Heavenly Father can never have too many children. He is willing and waiting to welcome any and every one of us home with open arms. So will you let Him?

Psalm 18:16-19

He reached down from on high and
took hold of me;
He drew me out of deep waters.
He rescued me from my powerful enemy,
from my foes, who were too strong for me.
They confronted me in the day of
my disaster,
but the Lord was my support.
He brought me out into a spacious place;
He rescued me because He
delighted in me.

PIGPENS AREN'T' JUST FOR PRODIGAL SONS! STUDY QUESTIONS

1. **Read Romans 12:2.** Are there areas in your life where you find yourself conforming to the world's expectations rather than God's? If so, list them.

Ask God to help you eliminate ungodly behaviors/relationships from your life. Ultimately, what/whom is better able to give you joy and satisfaction in life?

2. Like Kathy defended her boyfriend, even when faced with the truth of his destructive ability, do you "defend" sin in your life so you can justify keeping it around? Describe.

Read Isaiah 59:1-2 What does it say about how God reacts to continual and willful disobedience?

Is there a sin you are drawn back to over and over, that you lack the will to resist? If so, ask God to set you free from its enslaving power. Being free requires repentance—repentance is not just "feeling sorry" for what we have done, but also turning away from the sinful behaviors and turning toward God. Many times we do turn away from the sin, but do not RUN TOWARD God and we end up throwing ourselves into some other version of sin.

Freedom comes through repentance and also obedience. In John 8:31-32 Jesus says, "If you hold to my teaching, you are really my disciples. Then you will know the truth and the truth will set you free." What practical step can you take toward God (freedom) and away from sin (slavery)?

3. **Read Luke 16:13.** What does Jesus say about serving Him?

Many of us, if asked the question, "Who do you serve, who is your master?" would quickly say, "God." But do your actions, attitude, and time indicate that to be true? If others examined your life or walked beside you as if producing a documentary, would they come to the same conclusion or do your actions illustrate a different master? (worldly ambitions, kids, money, success, power, pride, a relationship, etc.) Who would people say your master is and why?

Thinking of idolatry usually conjures up images of golden figures and ritual sacrifice, but idolatry encompasses much more than those obviously evil things. Today it can be things as simple as television shows or food, or as life destroying as drugs or pornography (Colossians 3:5). It can even be "good" things like family, children, activity, work and the like. It is ANYTHING that comes between you and God—anything that you use to replace God's presence in your life. Anything you turn to INSTEAD of Him. Of course work and family and service and such are important parts of living a godly life, but if those things become the FOCUS of your life rather than God—you are involved in idolatry. Ask God to teach you how to live your life for Him instead of worldly things and relationships. Then watch how beautifully other relationships blossom as a result of inviting God's love to occupy that FIRST position in your heart.

4. Do you truly believe that God answers prayer?

What does James 5:16 say about the power of prayer?

Do you have unanswered prayer?

Do you feel God isn't listening to your prayers?

Write down any prayers you feel are not being answered.

Submit these prayers again in faith, knowing God does answer our prayers. Then trust Him to answer in HIS time and HIS ways. "In the morning, O Lord You hear my voice; In the morning I lay my requests before You and wait in expectation" Psalm 5:3. Let us wait expectantly for His answer.

CHALLENGE—return to this list each week or month to see if/how/when God is working. Be willing to praise God for any way He shows Himself—even if His answers don't match your desired outcome. This may end up teaching you something unexpected about your prayer life. God tells us that anything that we ask that is in His will, He will grant. Is what you are asking actually within His will? Is it something pleasing to the Lord? Sometimes we need to ask Him to change the desires of our hearts to match His before we lay our requests before Him. **Read Luke 11:9-13** for Jesus' discussion of asking for things (gifts) from God. He WANTS to pour out the Holy Spirit upon us. Just ask, seek and knock!

5. Looking back, Kathy is now able to see how God was at work in her life even when she refused to acknowledge His presence. Have you experienced God working in your life even when you were ignoring Him or rebelling? Briefly describe the experience if so . . .

Read Romans 8:28. How have you seen Him work good out of situations you hated or were sure couldn't be good for anyone?

God may be waiting for you to surrender a bad event or situation to Him so He can turn it into something good that glorifies Him and frees you. Are you willing to give it to God to handle?

6. **Read Romans 7:15-19.** Do you ever feel you, like Paul, are fighting against your own flesh, battling your own mind? What sins do you find yourself battling over and over? How do these relate to your answer from question one?

Read James 1:13-15.

Where does temptation come from? _____

After desire is conceived, it gives birth to what? _____

When sin is full grown, it gives birth to what? _____

Our sin comes when we allow ourselves to be dragged away and enticed by our own evil desires. We must battle it right there at the heart of its source.

What are some practical steps you can take toward conquering the fleshly desires and sinful thoughts that hinder your ability to obey?

EXAMPLE** The first thing Kathy did to step away from her fleshly desires was to simply pray for God to change her heart and desires.

7. Do you ever wonder if God has abandoned you? If you have been too sinful for Him to forgive?

Read John 10:28. If you have given your life to Christ then what promise is made to you?

Read Luke 15:11-24. The Parable of the Prodigal Son

Are you, like the prodigal son, longing for your Father's acceptance? Are you tired of rolling in the filth of your pigpen, trying to find satisfaction in the slop that the world tries to fill you with? One thing the Father won't do is force you to come back home. But when you do make that decision to leave your pen, He will, like the father in the story, see you and with compassionate arms open wide, allow you your place in His family. In verse 21, what did the son say to his father when he approached him?

Have you approached your heavenly Father in true repentance for your waywardness from Him?

What was the father's response to his son in verses 22-24?

Maybe you think God will allow you a place in His home, but only as a distant cousin or a workman low on the totem pole. That's not the picture He provides for us here.

Read 2 Corinthians 5:17-21

According to verse 17, if we are in Christ, we are . . .

We have been reconciled with God through Christ who, having no sin, became our sin on the cross so that one day we will stand before the Father completely clean. What an amazing thought, that no matter how much mud you have on you, God's grace can remove it all! And one day, we can all be seen by our Father, not dripping with filth and guilt, but completely clean!

If you HAVE NOT made that choice to invite Jesus into your life and follow Him, we urge you to consider His proclaimed gift in John 3:16 and make that choice now. He is waiting with open arms of forgiveness and love.

Notes:

JUST KEEP SWIMMING

Hurry! Pull her back!" I screamed as I ran to the shoreline.

Ryan was right on my heels as we reached the turtle. We both grabbed the slapping angry sea turtle and managed to successfully pull her back from the ocean. On land she was a bit clumsy and slow. She labored for each inch she moved. However, in the sea, her home, this sea turtle would become graceful and strong. It would be impossible to catch her then.

Ryan and I stretched out on the warm sand and watched our sea turtle begin to make her way laboriously back to the water's edge.

"It's a He," my brother remarked.

"No, it's my birthday, my birthday gift, and she is a girl!" I explained in response.

"Whatever, but he is getting very close to the water again. Is it your turn or mine?"

All that day we played with that poor turtle, our treasure. It was my tenth birthday. It was also the summer following my father's death. We took a month long vacation in the Bahamas. It became a time to reclaim our hope and to revive our spirits. For my brother and me, it was a time just to be children. For my mother, I think she found a way to leave the stress of that year for a while.

Our winter that year had been very serious and sad. In January, on my brother's birthday, my father died in a tragic accident at work. It was a shock to our family to say the least. In the days following his death as we were reeling from this devastating life change, many people came to visit. Friends, family, and even strangers began to tell us of times that my father had made a difference in their lives. It was often simple instances, "everyday things", that showed God's love. One man's visit stands out from the rest of the visits we received. Duncan and my father were co-workers. My father had spoken of him often. He had been witnessing to Duncan at work. My father's desire was to see Duncan come to know Christ. Duncan confessed to us that just following my father's death he had become a Christian. I remember him saying that my dad's death had been the catalyst that had caused him to make this decision. When you hear that someone has come to a saving knowledge of Christ, for Christians, it is often followed with acclamations of joy. I was a Christian at this time, yet I was not joyful at all. As a matter of fact, I was very angry. I thought, "You know if you had become a Christian just one week earlier, maybe my dad would not have had to die." My anger was pulling me away from seeking the refuge of God's comfort, just as my brother and I were pulling the turtle away from the water it needed to be in to survive.

You see my father was very serious about his faith. If asked, I have no doubt that he would have given his life for his friend. (John 15:12-13 *My command is this: Love each other as I have loved you. Greater love has no one than this that he lay down his life for his friends.")* Maybe, God had asked my dad to do just that and knew the desire of his heart . . . maybe that's why he died. To a nine year-old brain, this logic seemed accurate. Because Duncan had sinned, my father had to die. Because of Duncan, we were suffering unnecessarily. How in the world could he have waited until my dad had died?

So many questions plagued me . . . you see, I am a "question asker." I could not understand what was happening, so I questioned God . . . the only one who could actually answer these difficult wonderings. One of the most troubling questions began to come after my mom got remarried about five years after my father's death. My biggest question was, "Why was my dad dead when so many evil people were still allowed to be alive?

Let me explain why I began this line of questioning during this particular season of my life. After living with my stepfather for just a short time, we discovered that he was not the upstanding Christian man that he claimed to be. Out in public, he appeared to be kind and sincere. At home, in private, he was deceptive, controlling, and manipulative. We were emotionally and mentally abused, and even more.

My mom finally left this man after five years of a torturous marriage. The day she left was one of the most liberating days of my life (and I am sure hers as well). I finally felt safe and free. The divorce was not amicable and there was a lot of brokenness. I had developed a very close relationship with my stepsister. It was heartbreaking to have to leave her. There were tense financial stress points, and angry feelings, but the most outstanding feeling I remember from that time was complete relief.

At the end of their marriage I again began to ask, "Why does that man get to live and my dad had to die?" And then the other question of, "Why did my dad have to die just so his friend could live?"

Then it was God's turn to ask His question. In His quiet, calm voice, He began to ask me, "Was Duncan's salvation worth your dad's life? Is your life more valuable than someone else's life? Is or was your salvation worth My Son dying?" Well, I could only answer these questions honestly. I mean I was talking to the God of the Universe, He would have known if I was lying. My answer began, "I am a wretched sinner. I am not worthy of anything You are, or anything You have to offer. You sent Your Son to die for me. You sacrificed everything for me. I sacrificed nothing for You. I did nothing to deserve Your grace and forgiveness. You see, my dad, Duncan, my stepfather, and I were all unworthy. Only Jesus' blood makes us worthy.

With every question I could conjure, God already had the correct answer. None of the events of my life that had occurred were a surprise to God. He was using each and every moment of my life to shape me into a person who could better serve Him. He is God of the happenings of my life. And despite the fact that I was questioning His perfect way, God loved me. He saw deep into my heart and saw the blood of Jesus. He heard my questions and He answered them! *Mathew 7:7 "Ask and it will be given to you, seek and you will find, knock and the door will be opened to you.* I questioned the **God of the Universe** and He answered me!!! Just as He was drawing the turtle back to the sea, He was drawing me closer back to His arms. He heard my questions. He healed my grieving heart. He repaired my broken spirit. And then He restored my soul . . .

God is able to do far more than we could ever ask for or imagine. Ephesians 3:20 He has been so faithful to give me more than I could ever hope for or imagine including an amazing husband.

I just cannot begin to try and explain how perfectly Eric and I were made for one another. He is everything I am not, and yet we are so much alike. Eric is trustworthy and brave. He is logical and strong willed. These traits help him to compliment and sharpen many of my personality traits. *Proverbs 27:17 "As iron sharpens iron, so one man sharpens another."* Our marriage is a humorous combination of opposites attracting, two animals butting heads, and teammates helping each other win the Big game.

"I am really calling them. I am calling my parents. Shanelle, if you are not telling me the truth, you need to let me know now! I am dialing the phone. They are picking up. You're not kidding are you? Mom, Dad . . . you are going to be grandparents! We are pregnant!"

Eric likes for things to have plan. I fly by the seat of my pants. Needless to say, I was just a bit apprehensive when springing a pregnancy on him. For some married couples the next progression after marriage is children. For us, this was not supposed to be our future. I had been to the doctor just five months earlier and watched as his brow furrowed. "I really do not think you need to worry about birth control. With your medical history, it would be an absolute miracle for you to become pregnant. I just don't think it is possible."

At the age of two, I had been diagnosed with Cystic Fibrosis (CF). CF is a genetic disease that affects my lungs, digestive tract, and every other system in my body including the reproductive system. Cystic Fibrosis causes infections that are especially difficult to manage. The lungs can get damaged and nutrition, especially vitamin absorption, can be a problem. The result is usually poor growth, development, and sterilization. Not to mention the inability to support another human being. The lung infections are difficult to treat and can eventually lead to lung damage requiring lung transplants and even death. Traditionally, most CF patients did not parent children. Eric and I knew this and we were prepared for not ever having children. As a matter of fact, we had already been married for three years and had not ever used any birth control. It was not likely that I would ever get pregnant and if I did I probably would not be able to carry this child. For me to get pregnant with only one ovary and CF was nothing short of a miracle. One baby that was born healthy was an absolute miracle, but then two more followed! That gives you a glimpse of God's fantastic sense of humor. Just like He did for Job, He blessed me beyond my greatest expectations.

Through all of the trials, God had strengthened me. He challenged me at a young age so that He could make me into the woman I have become. He also blessed me abundantly. He has been faithful and He has been true to the promises that He made. *Psalms 119:65 "Do good to your servant according you your word, Oh Lord."*

I am a much better person having lost a parent. I never would wish it on anyone, but I know how faithful God is when He says He will comfort us. *Isaiah 49:13 "Shout for joy, O heavens; rejoice O earth; burst into song, O mountains! For the Lord comforts his people and will have compassion on his afflicted ones."* I grieved heavily for my father. At times I still grieve. And sometimes the grief is worse than it was at the age of nine. Grief changes as you age. I grieve for the loss of a spouse for my mother. I grieve for the loss of a confidant for my brother. I grieve heavily for the loss that it has made in my own life. I needed him to walk me down the aisle when I got married. I realized how much I needed him when my children were born. Sometimes I need spiritual guidance and I need to go to him. Even as a "big girl", I just sometimes miss having a daddy. And each time I grieve, I dive into the sea of God's love where He is there, loving me, listening to me, being everything I need from a father.

I am a better person because I lived with a dysfunctional stepfather. It took me the longest time to forgive him for everything that he had done. Many times I can still remember things and become angry. But it no longer pulls me back from seeking God's refuge. God understands. He comforts me and listens and heals my heart all over again. Then He allows me to forgive. And through this forgiveness He makes me whole.

I am a better person because of the opportunity to face a chronic illness each day. It is not easy. It is scary. I know that my life each day is a gift. When I am sick, it becomes painful and exhausting. It is not easy to imagine your children losing a parent just like you did. But then, God is there, loving me, listening to me, and promising that He will be there when I cannot.

In Isaiah 40:28-31, a race is described. If we trust in the Lord we will run and not grow weary, we can walk and not grow faint. When you run and walk you grow and strengthen muscle. Your heart develops and becomes healthier and stronger. When you are challenged by God to walk and run, He is trying to strengthen you. He is strengthening your heart. He is using your strong Christian walk for His Glory. He is asking you to trust in Him, and He is promising to help you. He is using your new, strong "trust muscles" for His Glory. *Romans 5:1-5 "Therefore since we have been justified through faith, we have peace with God through our Lord Jesus Christ, through whom we have gained access by faith into this grace in which we now stand. And we rejoice in the hope of the glory of God. Not only so, but we also rejoice in our sufferings, because we know that suffering produces perseverance; perseverance, character; and character, hope. And hope does not disappoint us, because God has poured out his love into our hearts by the Holy Spirit, whom he has given us."*

My brother and I fought all day with that stubborn sea turtle. We offered her our best food. We pulled her back from the surf more times than I could count. We tried to turn her around and confuse her. But all that turtle wanted was the ocean and she was doing everything in her power to go there. She was focused and unwavering. That turtle never lost her drive. She struggled, and fought and briefly tasted freedom time and time again. And finally she won. She fought a good fight and she won her race.

Isaiah 40:28-31

Do you not know? Have you not heard?
The Lord is the everlasting God,
the creator of the ends of the Earth.
He will not grow tired or weary,
and His understanding no one can fathom.
He gives strength to the weary
and increases the power of the weak.
even youths grow tired and weary,
and young men stumble and fall;
but those who hope in the Lord will renew their strength.
They will soar on wings like eagles,
they will run and not grow weary,
they will walk and not grow faint.

JUST KEEP SWIMMING
STUDY QUESTIONS

1. In Shanelle's story she uses the illustration of the poor sea turtle she and her brother kept trying to keep from the sea. The turtle knew the sea was her home, what sustains her. She wouldn't give up despite all their effort to stop her.

Have you been held back by life's circumstances, shame, doubt, or fear? What things keep pulling you away from a deeper relationship with God?

Take time right now to pray for God to remove that hindrance and give you the faith to trust Him completely.

Maybe you have been like Shanelle and her brother at some point—holding someone else back from their God-appointed goal so that you could have your own way. Though we may think we know what will make us happy, God sees the bigger picture and only when we are truly in His will and letting Him determine our life's course will we be truly happy. Take a moment to reflect on any way you might be holding someone back. Write it here.

If you aren't holding anyone back, wonderful! But if you are, what are some steps you can take toward letting that person reach their God-appointed goal?

In John 10:10, Jesus tells us "The thief comes only to steal, kill and destroy; I have come that they may have life, and have it to the full." Like the turtle, continue fighting toward the goal of a full life. Live in relationship with Jesus Christ regardless of the efforts against you and encourage others to do the same!

2. Think back to a time when you lost someone close to you. A broad range of emotions surface when we lose people that we love and care deeply about. For those of us who know our loved ones were Christians, we have the peace of knowing one day we will be with them again. However, even with the blessing of that peace, most people tend to experience difficult emotions such as anger, confusion, and helplessness.

Read Isaiah 55:8-9. What does the Lord tell us about Himself and how does this help you to understand your earthly circumstances?

Now read Isaiah 57:1-2. What insight does this give you into the mysteries of death and God's nature?

We may not ever have all the answers to why some of us are asked to bear such heavy loads. But God does give us purpose and hope in His very Word. **Turn back to Isaiah 55 and read verses 10 and 11.** Write what it says here in your own words:

There is much power in the Word of God. His Word never goes out and returns empty. If you are thirsty for something that cannot be satisfied by what this world has to offer go to the Word. Drink from the only water that will never run dry!

3. Jesus, God's only Son, came down to us, humbling Himself in the form of a man, to die for us. He knew His purpose and willingly, deliberately sacrificed Himself for each of us. He loves each of us so very much. **Read John 15:13 and 1John 3:16.** What does Jesus call us to do for one another?

Does it mean we have to physically die for someone?

_____

While some of us may be called into ministries that do actually put our lives on the line daily, most of us in the U.S.A. get to worship Christ without the fear of death. However, we are told in Romans 12:1 to "offer our bodies as living sacrifices, holy and pleasing to God—this is your spiritual act of worship." So while we may not ever be confronted with physical death in the name of Christ we are to die daily to our sinful selves so that Christ can live through us. In what ways have you died to your own desires to help serve others through Christ?

Is He asking you to give up something now to help another become closer to Him? What is it and how?

Do you believe others to be worth that sacrifice? Dear sisters, be encouraged : we are all worth it to Jesus!

4. Job is a famously troubled man in the Bible. The Lord allowed him to be tested because He knew Job would remain faithful. And thousands of years later, Job remains a quintessential example of faith and hope in adversity. We see in the beginning of Job that he was a very wealthy happy man. He soon, through no fault of his own, lost his children and land. He was inflicted with painful physical abnormalities and was getting no encouragement from his wife or friends.

As much as Job was made to suffer, he never waivered in his faith. He kept his focus on God knowing He is always a just and good God. Did he cry out to His Father God? Of course he did. God wants us to lean on Him, cry out to Him with our concerns and questions. However, we must be ready to accept any answer He gives us . . . even if sometimes the answer is "yes my child you must endure this hardship. Stick with me though and see how I will be glorified and how you will blessed." That's right, God didn't just leave Job suffering and wounded forever. When Satan realized that Job was not going to fold under the pressure of the most horrific events, he backed down. And God blessed Job many times over. **Read Job 42:12-13.** Write this scripture here in your own words.

What an encouragement to "hang in there" and stand firm. God has blessings just waiting to unleash on us but we must, like Job, keep our focus on God, not wavering in our faith. He is the ultimate deliverer and He will bless us for our faithfulness.

Job has been an example for many generations. Not knowing the plans God had ahead of Him he chose to stay the course anyway. We too are called to faith in God whether we know His plans or not. What areas do you have the most difficulty entrusting to God? Your health, spouse, children, career, etc? What keeps you from giving those areas completely over to God's control?

Maybe you feel as though you are in the midst of a terrible testing phase now. What are some of the ways you can follow in Job's footsteps in order to ensure you will still be standing in the end?

It's never too late for God. Maybe you feel like you have been dealt a pretty tough hand when it comes to your life. We encourage you to read all of Job's story. Most of us will never have to suffer the types of things that Job had to endure. But God didn't just leave him there. If you are still breathing then you still have time to be blessed. Is it possible you are already being blessed and are simply blinded by your suffering? Don't count God out just yet. Count your blessings instead! Maybe you have a home to live in, food to eat, a job to support yourself/your family, a family, a spouse, children, a supportive group of friends, good health, Jesus Christ's salvation, any number of things! Be thankful! Take a moment to list at least 10 blessings here . . .

5. **Read Acts 16:22-25.** Where were Paul and Silas?

What did they do while they were there?

Who was listening?

Paul and Silas rejoiced at being counted worthy to suffer for Christ. We can and are called to also have a faith strong enough to be able to rejoice in Christ even in the midst of great tragedy. It can be the greatest witness we are ever called to bear and have the greatest fruit! During difficult times consider doing some of the following:

- Remember Christ's suffering regularly (Mark 15:25-41)
- Understand how God uses all things for the good of those who love Him. (Romans 8:28)
- Remember how deeply our relationship with Christ can grow during trials. (Romans 8:17)
- Read your Bible daily. This is most likely when we will find His direction. (2 Peter 1:19, Psalms 54:4)
- Pray continually (Philippians 4:6-7, Matt 26:41).
- Praise Him anyway. Form a "holy habit" of praising Him always in all situations (remember Paul and Silas)
- Remember how much God really loves you! (John 3:16)

In Living Beyond Yourself, a study written by Beth Moore, she states, "Paul's joy in tribulation was motivated by his knowledge that the best of God's presence, purpose, and power was undoubtedly discovered in the worst of circumstances."

God seems to show us more of Himself when we are in the roughest of times. Joyfully praise Him in the midst of your trials so that others around you will be able to see the presence, purpose, and power of the Almighty God.

6. **Read 1Corinthians 9:24-27.** What metaphor does Paul use to illustrate our relationship with Christ here on earth?

We are all in the race. Whether we decide to invest ourselves in the worldly race, which consists of the treasures we can store up here on earth, or in the race for the ultimate prize—our spot in heaven and the treasures we will be able to give back to the one who gave us everything—is up to us.

Think about some of the things a world class runner or swimmer must do to finish a long race well. Then use the chart on the following page to write down some of the ways you can apply these same training strategies to your spiritual life and running the race God has called you to run.

Athlete's Regimen	Spiritual training applications
Train daily.	
Take in what is good for the body.	
Put the goal of winning ahead of other things in her life.	
Remain focused.	
Endure and manage pain.	
Set her sights on the highest goal for motivation.	
Listen to wise counsel of an experienced coach.	
Stretch to keep muscles healthy and flexible.	
Make personal sacrifices in favor of the goal.	
Take time for rest.	

One day the race will be finished for all of us. Will you cross the finish-line knowing you ran the race well using all resources given to us by Christ? Or will you be a runner no one ever notices who does just enough to be able to say they crossed the line? Let us run in a way that will excite others and entice them to join along with us!

TRUST AND OBEY

Many years ago in a small country church, a six-year-old girl was sitting on the front pew of a small Baptist church, half listening to the preacher and half thinking about Who God was. Someone sat down beside her and put His arm around her shoulder and said, "I want you to serve Me."

I knew it was Jesus and I said "yes."

As the days passed I began to do my Bible study. As I read my Bible, I found scripture which said to pray in your closet in secret. So I hid my Bible and a flashlight in the back of my closet and made myself a place to worship in secret. My parents had not a clue. For over a year I told no one because it was my secret place that I shared with Jesus. I had a strong foundation given to me through my parents who instilled a love for missions in my heart, leaders of the church, and my own desire to know Christ more.

Even with such a rich and steady foundation, I still faced many problems after I graduated from high school. There were times I felt that God had left me; yet in the midst of it all, I knew that God was in control. I took full responsibility for all that I did or did not do during that time and God and I spent hours sorting through it to help me find peace. I may have left God, but He never left me. For example, God blessed me with a man who would become my partner both in love and in ministry.

About two years after we married, our first child was born, thus beginning our journey as parents raising children in the ways of God. A year after our first child was born, we found out a second bundle of joy was on the way. Three months into that pregnancy, I went to the OB/GYN and the doctor could not hear a heartbeat. He told me the pregnancy would have to be aborted. I answered him with a resounding, "No way!" The doctor agreed to wait two weeks to be sure, telling me it would probably abort itself anyway. I said that if it is God's will so be it, but that is the only way. During that two weeks, I had been put to bed and I was told to stay off my feet. It was Sunday night and my husband and son had gone to church when I began to hemorrhage. In my mind I was afraid of the unknown and as I lay on the bed, I prayed. God this is your child. If you want it to come home and be with you now, take it, but if you desire for it to serve you here, I am ready to raise it according to your plan. The bleeding stopped immediately.

A month after her due date I was induced and she finally made her appearance . . . She. Did. Not. Breathe. As I lay on the table my mind went back to a night that I was bleeding profusely and God stopped it. I knew the baby would be fine. Time had passed and the doctors were ready to give up when, at last, she began to breathe. According to the doctors that was a miracle. The pediatrician came early the next morning to let me know what was happening and to take me to the baby. This beautiful baby girl would be retarded. She would do everything slowly. We were never to expect her to do normal things, much less, push her to excel. Her PKU test had proven that she was retarded. I looked the doctor in the eyes and said, "God is in control. My baby is normal. He has a plan for this child and she will be fine." My husband and parents were told that I was in denial.

Then after 3 months another PKU test was done, only this time it showed what I had known all along, that my baby girl was normal. Praise the Lord! The doctor said, "It is a miracle". This child that doctors wanted to abort and testing showed was retarded went on to graduate from college with a degree in teaching. I pondered all these things in my heart and remembered God's promises to me.

Both children were dedicated to God for His glory. This means my husband and I dedicated ourselves to providing a Christian home, Christian training, and a church home for our children to grow up in the admonition of the Lord. Anything good that would come from the kids would be God given. By God's grace and patience, both children did well.

When my oldest son, Tom, went to kindergarten, he was so excited, but I walked out of the classroom with tears in my eyes. My baby was growing up. I prayed and God smiled and said "He is mine and I am with him." How thankful I was that my heavenly Father could be everywhere. That statement would be the rock I stood on for a long time as God would ask me to release my children to Him over and over again.

About five years later at Ridgecrest Baptist Assembly in North Carolina, sitting on a back row of the auditorium for convocation, the Lord sat down beside me and touched me on the shoulder. He said that he wanted me to teach adults about missions and, "I want you to go home and tell your husband that, when the time comes, your child will be called to Southeast Asia to serve Me. You are to be an encourager. You are to tell only Tim." With tears flowing down my face, I said, "Yes, Lord".

Then came that time that every parent looks forward to but is scared to reach . . . our first born would go away to college. All kinds of scenarios could be imagined. I prayed for him daily and for every evil to be removed from him. He became a part of a discipleship group where he was discipled and later discipled others. His sister followed in his footsteps.

Indeed, after graduation our son Tom was led to Bangkok, Thailand as a missionary on a college campus. But I was not prepared for my daughter's news of wanting to go to Colorado for a summer missions program. She was only a sophomore in college and I had not yet heard from the Lord on this matter. That night my daughter and I cried most of the night as we struggled with my daughter's call. How would she get to Colorado? What had led her to think she should go? Where was the money coming from? Over and over the questions came and her pat answer was, "Mama, God called me and He alone will provide". No matter what was said, I did not have a peace about it. I hated the thought of leaving my daughter and going home without knowing what God's plan for her was.

As I got on the interstate driving my big conversion van, guess who decided to pay a visit? None other than our Lord and Savior, Jesus Christ, took the wheel and began a conversation with me. WHO'S VAN IS THIS? You provided it. SO IT IS MINE. Yes. I REALLY WANT YOUR DAUGHTER TO GO TO COLORADO. SHE WILL GROW IN MY WORD AND MINISTER IN MY NAME THAT I MAY BE GLORIFIED. I WANT HER TO GO IN MY VAN. SHE WILL BE FINE AND CAN HANDLE THE RESPONSIBILITY. I WILL BE IN CONTROL. I said, "Yes, Lord, as you desire". So, one child went to Colorado and the other prepared to go to Thailand.

Tom met and married the woman God had prepared just for Him. Molly and Tom's wedding was an answer to a mother's prayer. The night after the wedding, Vicki, our younger child, came to our motel room. She shared that her leg had a knot on it and that it was in pain. She said it had hurt so badly during the wedding she could hardly stand up. We tried to get her to go across the street to the hospital, but she refused. She did see a doctor when she returned to her college town who thought it would be fine.

With that prognosis Vicki was preparing to go to Thailand to spend a summer working on a college campus sharing the love of Jesus. Mother's Day she came home from school and her leg was still hurting. I told her I wanted an x-ray of her leg for Mother's Day. The two of us went to the Med-stop to see a doctor. He did x-ray it but thought I was being a little over protective. Vicki went back to school, but the next day the doctor called and told her to see the internist immediately. Tim, her father, made the trip to meet her and a friend the next morning because she was not to drive. The x-ray was picked up from the Med-stop for the appointment with the internist at 9am. At 10am the family was on the way to the orthopedic doctor and by 11 am an MRI was being done of her leg. At noon we got the news that Vicki was to go to Emory in Atlanta to a specialist the next day. It appeared the knot was a malignant tumor and the specialist in Atlanta confirmed the diagnosis.

And yet, Vicki told him to get her ready to leave for Thailand. He tried to tell her that might not be possible, but she was not listening. Surgery for a biopsy was scheduled for that week and things were moving very fast. The biopsy revealed osteogenic sarcoma of the right tibia and a regiment of chemotherapy was scheduled to begin immediately. Vicki said, "Not so fast, I am going to Thailand." She was prepared and willing to go, but she had to be prepared and willing to stay. Chemotherapy began with 16 weeks of treatment. During that time she would have the treatment for several days in the hospital and go home for a day or two, then reenter the hospital because her blood counts were too low to live in the normal world. Counts would build back up; she would go home a day or two and then back for the next round. Then it was surgery to remove the tibia, knee, and part of the upper bone. This was replaced with a titanium rod and knee. After surgery she had to learn to walk again and crutches became her best friends. She named them William and Mary.

Having gone through chemotherapy and surgery, the chemotherapy began again. This time it was really hard on Vicki. During the next months she would spend most of her time in the hospital, but never did she feel that God was not using cancer to bring others to Christ or that she would not get well. The hospital became her mission field. She returned to college to finish her last classes and back home where she did her student teaching. Vicki passed her state teaching exam with flying colors. She only missed two questions! She was ready to teach.

Every three months Vicki was having a scan to check for reoccurring cancer. It was time. At Crawford Long Hospital, the doctor said a place in her lung looked suspicious and more tests were scheduled. Eventually surgery to remove three tumors in her lung was performed. The surgeon came out and asked for us. His news was that surgery was over; however, there was a place where the aorta ran very close and they weren't sure if it had touched the malignant site. He did not want Vicki to know.

Vicki came through this surgery and was preparing to teach school when she began to have a cough and pain in her chest. More tests revealed the cancer had spread to her heart and she went to see the oncologist, who was not a Christian. He sat down with Vicki and me, looked her in the face and said, "You are going to die. You have less than six months". She said "That is OK; I know where I am going to spend eternity, where are you going to spend it?" He stood up with tears in his eyes and walked out the door. About 15 minutes later he returned and grabbed her, hugging her with tears streaming down his face. Vicki told him for her to die was fine as long as she knew she would see him in Heaven. What a day!

Vicki, whose mother had been told to abort her, was taking as many people to Heaven with her as possible. The days ahead could have simply been the hardest days of our family's life; however, God also made it the sweetest. Tom and Molly returned to the US to stay until Vicki went home to heaven. Tom and the deacons anointed her with oil and prayed for God's will. God's will was for her to spend eternity with Him in Heaven. It was not our will for this to happen at this time, but it was not our choice. Vicki belonged to the Father and we had given her back to Him at her birth. As parents, we do not own our children, though we are responsible for them. She belonged to Him. What a blessing.

Soon it was Christmas; three days after Christmas it would be Vicki's birthday and fifteen days later she would go home to be with the Father. She planned her funeral. One of the hardest things for a mother to do is to help a child plan her own funeral, but the Father made it so special. Vicki was looking forward to walking the streets of gold with Jesus and eventually seeing Mrs. Noah. She really wanted to know how she kept the ark clean. Her doctor made the trip from Atlanta to be at the funeral and on his way out of the church told my husband and me that because of our daughter he would see her again in heaven. What a blessing!

Tom and Molly returned to Thailand, where two of our grandchildren were born. His ministry was to train the nationals and he did, working himself out of a job. While on furlough in the United States, the Lord called his family to serve in a church as a mission pastor and he answered that call.

When God called that six-year-old little girl, little did I know what His plan for my life would be, but I knew that I was to follow him and trust Him with all that I was and all that I had. I made a lot of mistakes along the way, but God forgave me and used me. How does a mother go through the death of a child? Only through the mercy and grace of the Lord can you find the peace and joy to say thank you for cancer, thank you for taking my child to heaven. After all, is that not what I committed to do as I dedicated my children to the Lord? It has been eleven years since Vicki died. She is missed, but our family would never ask her to come back.

Our God is an awesome God. He prepares us through the bumps in the road for the mountain we must climb. He alone knows His perfect will for our lives. As a parent, the greatest gift you can give your child is to be an example of Jesus. None of us are good enough. None of us on our own can accomplish this task, but when we completely give it to the Father, He can. How do you give your children over to the Lord even to death? It is a daily walk with Him. It is a time of devotion every day where you read His Word and listen to the still small voice that is speaking to you. When your children are young it is hard to have time, but if you rise early before your day normally begins you will have time. God will wake you up. He desires to spend time with you. Realize along the way you are not perfect, your children are not perfect and if they make a mistake it is not your fault. They have the choice to make. Expect great things from them. Expect great things from the Father.

God called both of my children to serve Him. One serves as a minister of the gospel to people all around the world. The other He called to serve Him through her death on Earth, and her everlasting life with Him in Heaven. What joy floods my soul when I know the greatest gift was Jesus! Why not give Him your children? He knows everything. He knows exactly where they are, what they are doing, and what He desires them to do. Let Him have His way with you and your children. It may not be easy, but it is worth every step taken. When we are raising our children we want them to accept Jesus so they can spend eternity with Him, so when they do go to spend eternity with Him, rejoice! He will take care of you if they go to Heaven, if they go to a foreign mission field, or wherever He sends them.

I continue to trust God with my children. Tom gets on an airplane about once a month to another country to spread the gospel. Do I have fears? The answer is yes, but every fear is given to the Father. Every pilot and plane he rides is lifted in prayer. My God is sufficient to meet the needs we have. Vicki is in heaven with the Father. In God's time it will be only a twinkling of the eye and I will join her there. What our relationship will be when I arrive, I do not know, but I do know that it is in the very capable hands of the Father.

God has a plan and a purpose for my life. He is not through with me yet. It is my prayer that as you read this you will see that no matter what you are going through today, God is the answer and that He alone will provide. I know because He proves it over and over. The problems of life become small in the Master's Hand. Give Him your hand today. If you know it is Jesus asking, say YES!

TRUST AND OBEY STUDY QUESTIONS

1. Leigh had a very powerful and memorable salvation experience. She expressed her excitement so intensely. Recall your own experience of giving your life to Christ if you have made that decision. Describe the feelings you had at that moment of acceptance.

One of the best ways to share the love of Christ is simply to share what He has done in your own life. Take a moment now to write a 2-5 minute version of how Jesus has changed your life. Remember to focus on Jesus! (you may need a separate sheet of paper)

(If you aren't sure whether you have made that decision to follow Christ or are sure you haven't, please skip this question and go to page . . . . 115.)

2. If you are a Christian, once you were saved, did you then engage in biblical study to develop your faith and understand God's love on a deeper level?

Shortly after giving her life to Christ, Leigh began studying the scriptures and found meaningful truth to apply even at such a young age.

Read Matthew 6:5-6

After reading this, Leigh went immediately and made herself a prayer closet, a place just for her to spend time with her Savior. Do you take the Word you read and apply it so deliberately in your own life? Describe some ways in which you have taken scripture and made concrete practical applications in your daily living.

3. When our lives line up with God's will, He can ignite a passion within us that can set the world on fire, impacting generations to come. Many people impacted Leigh's life as she grew in her Christian walk, including her mother. Through her story you see how the fire for missions was passed from her mother, to her, and then to her children. When we are passionate about something, that passion spreads even to our children and beyond. What are you passionate about? What are you passing down to the next generation, whether it be your children, friends' children or the children and youth at your church? What would others say you are passionate about and does that answer satisfy you?

Take a moment to fill out this chart—listing things you want to pass down and those you believe you ARE passing down.

Things I want to pass down:	Things I am actually passing along:

Hopefully God has given you a passion that you are actively passing along. If you find that your lists are matching up, you are on the right track—don't let that fire be extinguished! If you find that they are not matching up as well as you would like, you may want to take some time to pray and ask God to show you how to prioritize what is most important. It may be helpful to have a close friend look at your lists and help you see more clearly.

4. Even if you are already familiar with the story of Shadrach, Meshach, and Abednego, take a few minutes **to read the story again in Daniel chapter 3.**

What were the three men called to do by the King?

In verses 16-18, what was their response to the King?

What were the consequences for that response?

How was God glorified in this situation because of their obedience to Him rather than man?

Sometimes we are faced with circumstances that require us to choose whom to believe. In Leigh's case, she was told by rational and "expert" medical professionals to abort her child and that the child would never have a good life. Leigh chose to listen to God's wisdom instead of that of man. Just like Shadrach, Meshach and Abednego, Leigh walked into the furnace and was met by God.

Are you willing to follow God even if it means being thrown into a "furnace"?

5. **Read 1 Samuel chapter one.**

What had Hannah so troubled in Chapter one?

What was Eli's first reaction to seeing her praying with such deep emotion?

When he discovered her true purpose, what did he do? And what happened?

Most times we are called to quiet, solitary prayer, but there are times when God calls us to pray no matter who is watching and perhaps because of who is watching. Sometimes we seem to be afraid to pray like this because others may see us as silly or attention grabbing, but when we bring our hearts fully before the Lord, others have the opportunity to not only see genuine prayer, but to join in. There is power in prayer and power in praying for one another.

What was Hannah's response in verses 27-28?

Hannah loved her son and she loved God. Her actions prove she loved God more. She trusted God and knew that her son ultimately belonged to Him and in His care, her son would be exactly who he was created to be. In fact, her son Samuel ended up being one of the greatest prophets in the Old Testament and had the privilege of anointing David as King.

In Hannah's position, how difficult would it have been for you to leave your son at the temple and only see him once a year?

Read 1Samuel 2:1-11.

How was Hannah's attitude toward God after leaving Samuel at the temple?

God may never call us to literally give our children over to the "temple" in a physical way, but we must be willing to give them over to God's service however God sees fit. He may ask them to remain close to home or He may send your child off to the other side of the world in a dangerous environment. The choice is God's and it is ultimately your child's decision to follow or not. Samuel may never have known the privilege of anointing the most famous and beloved King of Israel if his mother had not so willingly handed Samuel back to the Lord. As parents we are to teach our children to follow the call of Christ, and not succumb to the fears of what may be as a result of that call.

Leigh willingly dedicated her children to Christ at an early age and then forged in them a love for following Jesus that gave them the confidence and trust in the Lord to follow His every call.

In what ways are you praying for your child or the children in your life?

Ways you may want to pray—Are you praying for their salvation and/or their relationship to Christ to grow? Are you praying for their future/current spouses? Are you asking God to provide them with godly friends? Are you asking Him to use them in whatever way He deems prudent or are you asking Him to use them in ways YOU see as "good"? If your child is lost or in a rebellious phase, have you given him/her over to Christ, knowing that ultimately it is the power of the Holy Spirit that brings conviction of sin and then redemption through Christ?

6. There are many different ways God may ask you to give your children over to Him. Take a moment to think and pray over this. List some of the ways God may ask a person to relinquish their child over to Him:

What are some of the ways you have already had to give your child back to the Lord?

If God truly asks the difficult from you, as He did from Leigh, will you still be able to praise Him and will your answer remain "yes, Lord"?

***Challenge verse **Deut. 6:6-9:** These commandments that I give you today are to be upon your hearts. Impress them on your children. Talk about them when you sit at home and when you walk along the road, when you lie down and when you get up. Tie them as symbols on your hands and bind them on your foreheads. Write them on the doorframes of your houses and on your gates.

In what practical way can you immediately start putting this into practice? Name one thing you can do to act on it this week.

Matt 7:11—If you, then, though you are evil, know how to give good gifts to your children, how much more will your Father in heaven give good gifts to those who ask him!

Hebrews 11:1—Now faith is being sure of what we hope for and certain of
what we do not see.

Psalm 27:14 Wait for the LORD;be strong and take heart and wait for the
LORD.

SUFFICIENT FOR THE DAY
IS ITS OWN TROUBLE

Therefore do not worry about tomorrow, for tomorrow will worry about its own things. Sufficient for the day is its own trouble." Matthew 6:34

I have many verses underlined in my Bible and several marked with a star! I am proud to be a follower of our Savior Jesus Christ. My heart is to serve Him in ALL I do and with all of my heart. Our God in heaven, out of His amazing love, sent His only son to die for our transgressions (John 3:16). This seems so incomprehensible! He has made my life complete and He has carried me through many valleys. Oh, how I can name the miracles He has done in my life even as a young adult when I was NOT following Him! But, amazingly and to my dismay, I still find myself being consumed by fear and worry. Perhaps this is why Matthew 6:34, in particular, has received double stars AND been underlined. Worrying comes very naturally to me; even as a little girl I remember believing I could "magically" control the outcome if I mull over whatever it may be. I struggle with needless fretting to this day (age 40).

Just today, in my daughter's health book, the emotional issues were discussed. It mentioned that "Fear not . . ." is in the Bible 365 times—one for each day of the year! (Michele—listen!) Worry is really FEAR and fear is not of God. Satan knows my Achilles heel. Sometimes I dream of what it would be like not to worry, not to even think about what might happen tomorrow. Imagine the serenity of Heaven—I will not be worrying!

Meanwhile, here on earth, in my mortal body, developing faith has been a process. The Lord has brought me a long way in the past 10 years—but I definitely have more work to do! The Lord is so good to wait patiently for me to finally quit thinking about whatever the care is of the day—and hand it over to Him! I picture Him waiting quietly with His hand outstretched—waiting for ME to grab it! HE is always there! I often look to the Psalms for comfort and guidance. Psalm 61 has been scripture I look to many times. *"Hear my cry, O God; Attend to my prayer. From the end of the earth I will cry to You when my heart is overwhelmed. Lead me to the rock that is higher than I . . ."* (I love to think of David crying to God just as I do—and he's DAVID!)

"The name of the Lord is a strong tower; The righteous run to it and are safe"
(Proverbs 18:10)

"He is my rock and my salvation; He is my defense." (Psalm 62:6)

"For You have been a shelter for me, a strong tower from the enemy . . . I will trust in the shelter of your wings." (Psalm 61:3)

My God, your God, has infinite wisdom and power. He desires our love and relationship. He promises He will protect us and care for us.

Excruciating circumstances often bring about the most growth in us. As a newly baptized mother of a beautiful 4 year old daughter and 2 year old son, my husband and I received devastating news. I'll never forget that moment when we were told our son has a heart abnormality and will require open-heart surgery in the future (Can you say F-E-A-R?) The future, it turns out was a year later. As a new Christian this was a huge lesson in trust for me. I had to hand our sweet little boy over to have MAJOR surgery. I could feel God in a way I had never felt before—He was so tangible. God's comfort and love enveloped me—I was actually very calm during surgery—peace that surpasses understanding! For me, a true worrier, to be at peace was only through HIM!

"Do not be anxious about anything; but in everything by prayer and supplication with thanksgiving, present your request to God. And the peace of God, which transcends all understanding, will guard your hearts and your minds in Christ Jesus."
Philippians 4:6-7

As I look back, I realize what a huge lesson I learned—the lesson of true faith and trust. Although I would never wish this upon my son, I praise God for what He has demonstrated through this situation.

"Peace I leave with you, my peace I give you. I do not give as the world gives. Do not let your heart be troubled, and do not be afraid." John 14:27

My dear son's life has been an exercise in learning to trust for me. The "one time" surgery left him with a damaged valve which must be closely monitored. He has been scheduled for 2 more subsequent surgeries, but our AWESOME GOD intervened in both cases and He did not have them. My son's activity level does not fit with what the doctor sees in the cardiac testing! This child with a heart condition has ridden a 34 mile bike ride (probably not many 11 year olds can say that!) and God has worked miracle after miracle in his life!

The last time he was scheduled for surgery, we actually got to the point of being admitted to the hospital, where our son was preparing to have surgery. The anxiety leading up to this point touched every part of my life. The decision to put him through surgery was an agonizing one. The doctors felt it was time. I could not stop thinking about what my son was about to endure and how I would be able to handle the situation. Satan continuously threw "what ifs" at me. What if he didn't undergo surgery, would something bad happen? Or if he did have surgery: What if something went wrong? What if he was getting sick and we didn't know it? What if the surgeon found more wrong? Oh, this was a very difficult time for me. The possibilities, no matter what our decision, seemed too much for me to handle. Would I ever have peace?

So, there we were in the hospital, my son had been hooked up to a heart rate monitor, hospital gown on and beginning pre-op. After a quick examination and speaking with us, the surgical team had met to discuss our son's surgery. The head surgeon and his team came back into the room to tell us what they felt was the best course of action. (My son's heart condition is not an easy situation to assess—there are several possibilities depending on what they see once inside.) I will never forget that moment when the surgeon looked at us and said they wanted to tell us the best plan of action at this point is for our son to go HOME! Jubilant is not a strong enough word for how we felt! (Our son was about to receive his IV—God even relieved him of ANY procedure!)

We serve an awesome God who can do ANYTHING! (Why do I forget that at times?) We knew the Lord worked through our surgeon that day—I felt the Lord's presence in that room. I am so thankful for the power of God and for the surgeon who was an instrument for a miracle! One of the nurses said being sent home at that point was extremely rare! This was a defining moment for me—finally after 6 years my heart KNOWS the Lord is in control of my son's heart problem (of course He was all along!)

My entire family has grown through my son's heart challenges and this situation has touched many, many people. God's ways are not our ways—but He knows how to "do it big!" The moment we were told we could go home—my husband and I grabbed my son and just cried tears of joy. Our 7 year old son cried as well—he knew at this young age what it meant to be relieved of surgery. He saw first-hand the power of God and power of the prayers of believers. One of those so faithful was my husband, who felt all along that the Lord would not have our son go through surgery. The most special moment that day is when my husband looked our son in the eyes and said how much he had prayed for him and for a miracle! Our son is a very contemplative, deep, and spiritual child, and his experiences have strengthened him as well. It will be exciting to see what God has in store for his life. God loves our children more than we do! He is also working in THEIR lives and strengthening THEIR walk.

Trusting God with our children is probably one of the most difficult areas for me. How could He possibly love them or protect them more than me? Well, in reality we have no power or control! Our Father in heaven possesses all power and control. Worry for me has been a form of control. Perhaps I can worry and have an impact on the situation (Ha Ha!). One of the ways I learned to trust God with our children was the decision to homeschool. My husband felt like we were to homeschool our daughter from the start, but I had to worry about the responsibility, about whether it was the right decision. Was I really capable of educating my children? Therefore my daughter attended kindergarten and first grade. During Christmas break her first grade year, the Lord made it very clear to me (or perhaps I finally listened) yes, we were to homeschool. It was difficult to pull her out—what would people think? I was worried our daughter's wonderful teacher (also friend) would feel it was because of her—we loved her being our daughter's teacher. What will my family think? What will my friends think? (they have all been very supportive, by the way!) *We ought to obey God rather than men . . ." Acts 5:29* Here we are 7 years later—continuing to homeschool both of our children. The opportunities we have had as a family have been wonderful! I thank God for allowing me to educate my children and to spend this precious, fleeting time with them. What a huge blessing it has been for our family! *"In You, O Lord, I put my trust. Let me never be ashamed." Psalm 31:1*

One of the greatest concerns I have in raising my children is their walk with the Lord. Am I doing enough? Have I told them all they should know? Should I worry about it? Who do I think I am? My 13 year old daughter told me on Mother's Day she was ready to be baptized and make a commitment to follow Jesus! I knew she had been contemplating the decision but she came to it on her own. How grateful I am that the Lord spoke to her heart! I have watched her grow stronger and stronger in her own faith—what a gift! This was another lesson of learning to trust our mighty God with our kids. We have the responsibility to train our kids according to God's Word, teach them about our Lord, help them along the life's path and pray for them. *"Train up a child in the way he should go, when he is old, he will not depart from it" Proverbs* 22:6 Our children must make their own decision to listen to the Lord's call on their life. The day my daughter chose to make the commitment to the Lord Jesus Christ will forever be in my memory! Thank you Lord for loving them more than I do!

The Lord continues to show Himself to me in amazing ways. In my emotional worry I have learned to go to Him in prayer. I'll wrestle for a while then finally hand it over. How humorous that I KNOW in my head I should hand it over, but it takes a while for my heart to follow.

"I will lift up my eyes unto the hills from whence cometh my help. My help cometh form the Lord, which made heaven and earth." Psalm 121:1-2

I love the illustration of Peter on the water with Jesus until he took his eyes off of Jesus! What must have been going through his head—worrying about what is going on around him. Keep our eyes on Jesus! No matter what! TRUST—NO WORRY—BELIEVE. While Peter's focus was on Jesus, he WALKED ON WATER! What a miraculous feat because of the power of God!

I believe with all my heart our Lord loves us, helps us to grow and performs miracles every day. The Lord leads and guides—we must listen. I have seen our family transform over the past 10 + years—going from occasional church attendees to being deeply involved in church and ministry (my husband is the music minister at church, our kids play worship music with him at times, I serve with him, we have a wonderful church family etc.) I believe that the Lord led us and strengthened us through many (and sometimes very difficult) circumstances—we MUST be bold for HIM and proclaim His greatness. Thank you Lord!

I thank the Lord for not giving up on me! I am thankful for all the opportunities He has given me to learn to trust Him. Also, for all that He has carried me through or situations He has calmed. I stand in awe of what He has done in my life! With the Lord's help, I will strive to be less of a "worrier" and more of a "warrior"! My heart's desire is to make an impact for His eternal Kingdom. Praise God!

"The Lord is my rock, and my fortress,
and my deliverer, my God, my strength,
in whom I will trust;
my buckler, and the horn of my salvation,
and my high tower."
Psalm 18:2

SUFFICIENT FOR THE DAY IS ITS OWN TROUBLE STUDY QUESTIONS

1.Define in your own words what worry is.

The Webster's definition of worry is "mental distress or agitation resulting from concern usually for something impending or anticipated."

When you are concerned about something, what are your thoughts like? Do you think over and over again about that concerning thing? What is your first reaction to troubling events? Do you pray, do you plan, do you act or do you worry?

The author states at the beginning of her story that worry came very naturally for her. For most of us worry is very natural whether it is over how we are going to fit in time to make it to the grocery store in an already busy day or over a life and death health problem we or someone we love gets diagnosed with.

What are some of your worries?

Now **read Mathew 6:25-34.** Write a brief summary of what these verses mean and how they speak to you about what place worry should have in our lives.

How would you rate yourself on being able to let tomorrow worry about its' own things?

/_____/_____/_____/_____/_____/_____/_____/
Don't worry   Obsess

2. Michele mentions that worry is really fear. Does worry keep us from (or is it evidence of not) trusting God as deeply as He asks us to?

Turn to Psalms 62:5-6. Fill in the blanks.

"Find _____, Oh my soul, in _____ alone, my _____ comes from _____. He alone is my _____ and my _____; he is my _____, I will not be shaken."

There is only one source of true rest for our souls and that is in God alone. When we are overtaken by fear and worry, no amount of worldly riches, no amount of therapy, no amount of anything can bring us the rest and comfort we need except God Alone.

Maybe you feel overwhelmed by life's concerns. What would happen if you chose to cry out to God in those times just as David, the writer of this psalm, did rather than attempting to "fix" things yourself?

The image of running into a strong tower or fortress for safety may be more familiar to some than others, but we can all imagine a flood or a storm coming and how we would feel if we were caught alone, out in the open with no shelter to run to. But so often we are in those storms and choose not to head for the shelter that is stronger than even the deadliest of storms. God wants us to run to Him. He promises protection and guidance and yet so often we think we need to try things on our own, only to find out we really will sink without the boat, fall without the protective wings of our Father to carry us.

Describe a time in your life when you were overwhelmed and chose to rely on your own wits and abilities rather than seeking the protective shelter of the Lord.

What were the consequences of "going it alone"? Did you ever come to the Lord to give over control?

3.**Read Philippians 4:4-7.** What does verse 4 say we are to do always?

It doesn't say rejoice only in happy joyful times it says ALWAYS. Verse 5 says "let your gentleness be evident to all." Gentleness here is described as Christ like consideration for others. Why do you think Paul added this line in here between verses 4 and 6?

Paul knew that it is because he knows that no matter what our circumstances we as Christians are being watched by others to see if we will lose our Christ like consideration for others when we face our own hard or trying times. Following this in verse 6 we are told to be anxious for nothing. It goes on to say we are to present our requests to God. How or in what manner and attitude according to verse 6 are we to bring our requests before God?

And according to verse 7 what will happen if we obey in the above ways?

4. Our God is indeed a trust worthy God and yet when we worry it is as if we are saying we don't trust God to take care of what is worrying us. When you worry you are displaying a belief that God's power has limitations. Read the following verses about trust:

Psalms 9:10
Proverbs 3:5-6
Psalms 37:3-4
Isaiah 12:2
Romans 15:13

According to the scripture what seems to happen for those who place their trust in our Heavenly Father?

When trying to decide whether or not to homeschool her daughter, Michele went through years of questioning, doubting, excuse making and fretting before finally enrolling her in school—only to figure out she really was supposed to homeschool. Do you ever find yourself trying out every solution, reasoning or excuse before giving it over to the Lord?

Sometimes we, like Michele, are not sure if what we are hearing is direction from God. But if we seek him it will eventually be made clear and we will have to make a decision to obey. Describe a time when you heard God's direction but either were unwilling to obey or simply did not recognize it as his instruction.

5. Michele experienced a great and miraculous peace during her son's heart surgery. What do you think that demonstrated to the people around her during that time—especially those close enough to her to know her as a worrier?

Why do you think most of us seem to be surprised when God answers prayer or performs a miracle? Why does it often take such a huge "sign" for us to understand that God is the One in control, always has been and always will be?

While many in the hospital room the day Michele's son was unexpectedly sent home and surgery cancelled felt God's presence and understood His role in the events, there were those who did not recognize the truth of God's working. They simply attributed these amazing events to "good doctors" or her son's level of exercise or to "coincidence" without acknowledging the amazing orchestration that had to come into play to make these things happen just as they did. Why do you think many people refuse to acknowledge God even when He is so clearly working?

Have you ever witnessed miraculous events and seen others dismiss them as coincidence or some other phenomenon? Have you ever been that person? Did you say anything to that person (or did anyone say anything to you) to try to explain God's sovereignty? What was the response?

Miraculous events happen around us all the time. When we are in tune with the Holy Spirit we are much more aware of God's miraculous work. Responding to these events as the miracles that they are gives us an opportunity to provide a bright reflection of the Light of this world, Jesus Christ. This week try to be aware of those daily miracles. Write them down and share them with someone.

Daily miracle list:

6. The root of worry or fear is self-centeredness. We worry because of how things may affect us or those we love or what others think of us and we fear because we think of ourselves and take our eyes off Jesus.

Read Matthew 14:22-32 and then turn back and read Matthew 8:22-27.

The disciples already had evidence of Jesus' vast power. Why then do you think they were so afraid?

What happened when Peter took his eyes off Jesus and looked at the wind and waves (circumstances) instead? Describe how that may happen to us.

How long after Peter cried out for help did Christ rescue Him?

Look at what Peter later says in **1 Peter 5:6-7**. What does that tell you about Peter and what can you take from it to apply to your own life?

7. Michele's life is a shining example of how our God likes to bring joy and peace to those who love Him, to those who continue following Him even in hard times. In 1 Peter 2:2-3 we are told that when we have tasted and seen that the Lord is good we are then to grow in Him as Michele and her family have done. List some ways you have tasted and seen that the Lord is good.

And now that you have seen that He is good "grow up in your salvation" showing everyone around you what it looks like to completely trust in your Heavenly Father to take care of you.

Take some time in quiet prayer. Ask God to show you areas in your life where you are worrying instead of trusting. Then list out ways in which you can begin or continue to grow up in your relationship with Him. Choose one to begin working on this week. Keep up with your progress and consider having someone hold you accountable and with you in this progress.

Some scripture for further study:

Psalm 34:4-9
Psalm 102
Psalm 77
Psalm 56
Psalm 61

DELIGHTED

I couldn't stop smiling for days. I had just met him that weekend and couldn't stop thinking about him. The grin wouldn't go away and I was doodling his name in my notebooks instead of taking chemistry notes. I wore his necklace so everyone would know we were together. I couldn't stop talking about him. I was in love with the most wonderful man. I was 15.

Growing up I had always been extremely shy and never really felt I fit in anywhere except at home. I was blessed with awesome parents and a sister, with whom I remain close. But it was outside, in the world with others, where I struggled. I am a stocky, we'll say "sturdy" person, unlike the lithe, thin girls I grew up with. In middle school (doesn't it begin here for so many of us?) I had some real trouble as several major negative events occurred. Some would be major to everyone, some just to a middle school aged girl, but all were major to me. I had always been introspective, but my thoughts began to turn a little dark. I questioned my worth, my very existence. I began seeing myself as ugly, as fat and worthless . . . inside and out.

I began the perilous descent into the slavery of an eating disorder at the age of 13. It started by giving away my lunch every day. I also discovered my athletic side and poured myself into exercise and sports. What a great release. That summer my body did some changing, as bodies tend to do at that age. All I saw was the weight change, not the young woman I was developing into. That first year of high school I stepped up my efforts to control my misbehaving body. When given an assignment for a paper in health class I chose anorexia for my topic. No one would suspect a thing—all the while I would be learning the "tricks of the trade"—mostly how to carefully conceal my actions from anyone else and how to lie, A LOT.

I had a tendency, from birth I think, to try to be the best at everything I did. I didn't ever really require external motivation. But as we all know, being THE BEST and doing MY BEST are two entirely different animals. I wanted to stand out somehow, to demonstrate to others and mostly to myself that I was special, worth something. Looking back I see that is a dangerous place to be. Being THE BEST is an elusive brass ring—there is always someone better out there—and our worth doesn't come from what we do, but from who we are. No really, from WHOSE we are. As much as I have tried over my lifetime to achieve greatness—or at least worthiness—I have never succeeded. Not on my own.

I went through years of SELF-hatred, SELF-punishment, SELF-denial, and was living in a SELF-imposed prison being so SELF-focused! As much as I had wanted to demonstrate love and set myself aside for others, until I met that love of my life at 15, it was ALL always about me. It made me sick when I realized it, but unfortunately I didn't realize it for YEARS.

Even in that first "honeymoon period" with my new love, it was about what he could do for ME, how he made ME feel, MY new life with him. He was SO amazing. How he came into my life and pulled me up by my heartstrings and started turning my head gently to his face—it makes me melt even now. Even in the bliss of a new relationship—or perhaps BECAUSE of it—I delved deeper into trying to make myself worthy for a while. At one point I had gone almost 3 weeks without food and ended up passing out at school and getting physically ill. So much for being secretive. I didn't think I deserved his love as I was. I still felt so out of control and so fat and unworthy. My heart was lifting but my mind was still a raging battleground. Finally, my best friend at the time apparently couldn't take it anymore (I hadn't been as secretive as I had thought). She told her mother what I had been doing and they both came to my house and, in front of me, told my mom what had been going on. I couldn't hide it anymore. My carefully constructed house of cards was toppling down over me. I was sent to therapy in a loving effort to try to help me overcome this unhealthy pattern. I hated it. I actually began turning my hatred and anger toward myself onto others, but before I could learn to actually handle and correctly place those feelings, I told my parents I was "fine" and wanted to quit therapy.

I lied. My love was gently ushering me to himself, offering love, acceptance, and healing and I was lying. Not just once here and there, but constantly. I hated myself for it, but I didn't see any other way. I HAD to punish my misbehaving body and mind, but I couldn't let on to others or they would try to stop me. My love was still waiting, beckoning me to let him hold me, let his love heal me. I had joy deep in my heart. At least I didn't want to kill myself anymore. And yet I still had to die . . . I just didn't know it yet.

Things were better the next year, my senior year in high school, until a good friend threatened to end our relationship if I kept on doing what I was doing—starving myself and making derogatory comments about myself. He made me FINALLY realize that things weren't all about me. I WAS loved. I WAS special. And I was hurting the very people I was trying to love with my self-destructive behavior. Within a few months I ceased starving myself and never did it again. I began to be quieter and listen—weighing my words. No more lies. It was a start.

I left for college during this time. Excitement. Fear. Opportunity. I met my husband when I was 17 at orientation. I was so blessed. I stopped the incessant busyness that characterized my life. I HAD to. I got mononucleosis soon after arriving to school and was pretty ill most of that first year. It was such a blessing! I had been given a beautiful gift—TIME! I could focus. I did very well academically without really even trying—making up for those lost years in high school. I got to be "the best" in my class without even realizing it was an option. I had been empowered in so many ways. I graduated and started teaching troubled high school students—a perfect place of ministry for me I thought. What another blessing. I only taught for 3 years but I am still reaping the fruits so many years later.

I left teaching to go back to school for a Master's in Marriage and Family Therapy—so I could "REALLY" help kids, ironically enough. I ended up doing very well in that program as well—even though the program tore out my insides and attempted to rebuild them. It couldn't do it, but at least I was brought down to my foundation. It was during this time I discovered that

I had left my love behind. He had given me a new life, love, joy, power and reason, and I had quit going to his house; I hadn't talked to him enough. I had begun to only look for his gifts, not him, and I didn't give anything in return. He had helped release me from my prison, freed me from the slavery of perfectionism and self-hatred, starvation and obsession. I thought I had somehow done it all on my own. Did I thank him? Did I live my life in devotion to my love? No. I began to realize how wrapped up in myself I had become . . . again . . . and I was sick, and so very guilty. I wasn't sure he would want me, but I started visiting him again and talking to him more often. My husband went along with it. He actually encouraged this relationship with this other love. He came to his house with me, talked to him as well. We had both pledged our lives to each other and to my love at our wedding ceremony. JESUS was beckoning us both into His arms. This Love I had met at 15, was still gracious and wants me, ALL of me, ALL the time.

My husband and I started going back to church—my Love's house—the place I had avoided in favor of finding my own way. The very environment which had led to that glorious romance with Christ was exactly where I hadn't wanted to be. (. . . "but they did not realize it was I who healed them. I led them with the chords of human kindness with ties of love; I lifted the yoke from their neck and bent down to feed them." Hosea 11:3b-4)

Several things changed that . . . slowly. A good friend I had met in grad school and her husband kept quietly inviting us to events with church people—not church necessarily. They even let us live with them a few weeks while our house was being finished. God sent them to us, as He had sent so many others all along to guide us toward Himself. So when my beloved nephew was scheduled for open heart surgery at the age of 3, we had been prepared a place to go. We had a place to take our fear and our pain and be lifted up. We have been attending that church ever since the February of my nephew's surgery. Christ was, and is, showing Himself through His people. I felt myself being drawn to Christ slowly, steadily. I was beginning to understand that I did need to die after all and how I needed to die—to myself. I needed to relinquish my life and desires to Him and let Him fill me—but I didn't know how yet. I began to pray a lot. I was learning truths about God in Sunday School, through choir music, and in sermons that I either hadn't heard before or simply hadn't listened to before.

My husband and I began taking a Henry Blackaby course taught by our pastor called "Experiencing God". That title was prophetic for me. During this time several very key things happened at once—pulling together my soul and bringing me full face to Christ. I was learning to hear from God and know His voice in the Experiencing God class and I had no idea just how personal that experience could be.

It was then that something happened that changed not only MY world forever, but the ENTIRE world forever. September 11, 2001 was a day neither I nor anyone else will forget. Like most, I remember exactly what I was doing when I heard that a plane had hit one of the towers and the shock, terror, and subsequent sick sense of grief I felt when they said another plane had hit and then one into the Pentagon and yet another crashed to the field in Pennsylvania. I had to work that day and did not see any of the images that brought the reality of the immense evil to me until the afternoon. It was then, with the television permanently etching the images of falling towers and people plunging to their death, in my mind's eye, that I knelt before God. I got down on my knees and prayed with a heavy heart for all those families and those that were suffering. But I was met with something, no SOMEONE, I didn't expect.

I found myself at the feet of my Savior, my Love. So unexpectedly and so undeserved—He was there with me—tangible, pure, holy and so full of love I couldn't look at Him. I wept and I cried out not with my voice, but with my very soul. I felt the weight of His hand on my bowed head as His silhouette was framed by a beautiful light and the conquered cross stood behind Him. He gave me love and comfort that broke me into pieces. My soul was leaping and my heart was sinking all at the same time. Here He was! Jesus! Right in front of me! Present! Here I was, deeply hurt, sorrowful, unworthy. I was no longer just weeping for our country or those poor people and their families that had forever changed that day. I was weeping for my own life, laid bare before the cross; crying from somewhere deep in my soul where there are no words. He was speaking to me with the touch of His hand and a gentle voice I didn't hear but rather felt deep inside me. Holding me in my grief for those I didn't even know and seeking me out as I grieved over my own sinfulness. My Love wasn't too busy, even though millions of others were calling to Him at that same moment. And I wasn't too insignificant to Him. (My Lover spoke and said to me "Arise, my darling, my beautiful one, and come with me" Song of Songs 2:10.) It was in this moment that the turn to Him was made by conscious choice.

I wanted desperately to remain in His arms that day, to be cradled like a babe in its Father's arms, safe, loved. His physical presence left me, but my soul is always searching Him out and His Spirit remains. This is the first time I truly dedicated my life to Him in full. I had never really been comfortable using the name Jesus before and telling Him I loved Him. That moment changed it all. I love Him so very much. My heart aches for Him. I bask in the light of the thought of being with Him one day for all time. It is a glorious morsel to savor—to roll around in my mind like a connoisseur tastes and savors an excellent new wine. It fills me when I think of it—and I am desperate for more of Him. "Taste of the Lord and see that He is good. Blessed is the man who takes refuge in Him." Psalm 34:8

Life since has been an amazing blend of daily (hourly) dying to myself; struggling to grow in Christ and fighting the temptations of this world; forgiveness; and blessings beyond measure. I do fight the tendency to get distracted, to be overcome by temptation and lose hope that I will ever be truly free. Satan likes to attack me in many ways such as with guilt, pride, comparison to others, hopelessness, ever-present temptation to "taste of the world" and, horribly, by sneaking doubts about my Love into my head. Admittedly and regrettably I cooperate many times, but Christ's Holy Spirit within me reminds me of my true Love and that He has forgiven me—I AM free and have His power within me to defeat the Enemy. Recently I read something from Beth Moore that said "freedom never comes through disobedience." How backward that seems—I have to obey to be free, but I find such precious truth in that. When I do make that daily choice to obey my Lord, I find that I am blessed and burden is lifted, rather than added.

I have been blessed with a husband devoted to Christ, two beautiful boys, opportunities for service and relationships with other lovers of Christ Jesus that have enriched my life deeply. Jesus, my Love, has revealed Himself to me in so many ways. Even in the midst of tough times, I can now see His Hand in things and how He is working for the good of all of us. Mostly, I am learning to trust Him, regardless of whether I understand His ways. I can't wait for our quiet times alone together and I am learning to sing praises to Him with abandon. He has even used me, imperfect, unworthy me, to bring others to Himself. I am blessed to be the object of affection in the greatest romance of all time. ". . . as a bridegroom rejoices over his bride, so will your God rejoice over you." Isaiah 62:5.

". . . My Lover is mine and I am His." Song of Songs 2:16a.

DELIGHTED STUDY QUESTIONS

1.Early in Valerie's story she talks about being self-driven and about how she was never satisfied with doing her best, only with being **the** best. Read Philippians 4:11-13. In the space below write down what the Bible says about being content.

Are you dealing with any unhealthy obsessions in your life caused by either your drive to be the best or just your inability to say no to a desire you know is unhealthy? List them.

Now, **read Philippians 4:8.** Here Paul is conveying that he understands the influence of one's thoughts on one's life. List those things Paul says to think about or focus on.

Whatever is occupying your mind will soon find its way to your speech and eventually your actions. "Think about such things." It was Paul's way of encouraging us to meditate or focus on the "Godly" things or the "Beautiful" things in our lives and around us so that our speech and our actions will soon reflect that beauty and Godliness. Finding contentment may not require us to become the best at something or perfect at anything. It may just be that we need an inward adjustment to be able to treasure what is really important in life.

2.) Do you measure your self-worth by comparing yourself to those around you?

Why is this dangerous to do?

Read Psalms 139:13-16. What does verse 14 tell us about how we are made? _____. After reading that scripture there should be no doubt of your worth to our Lord. We are all precious to Him and we are all created for a purpose given to us by the one who created us. He has loved each of us since the time we were first "knit together" and He made us all different so that we could fulfill the lives in which He created us to live. Comparing ourselves to those around us is not a true measurement of our self worth. It only hinders us from reaching our true potential.

3.) Valerie mentions having a Christian friend who was willing to take a chance of ruining a friendship in order to help save Valerie's life. Do you have any Christian friends in your life that would be willing to do the same? If so, list them and take a moment to thank God for them!

Read Ecclesiastes 4: 9-12. If you don't have a Christian friend that you can lean on in hard times as well as rejoice with in good times, seek one out. Pray that God will send you a special companion in your walk with Jesus to encourage you and make you stronger. (Proverbs 27:17) Surround yourself with women who love God and who love you and are willing to tell you the truth even when they know it will hurt.

Take a moment to write a prayer asking God to bring a Godly woman into your life that encourages you in a friendship founded and built in Christ. Thank Him for the ones you may already have.

4.) Many women will either never come to a relationship with Christ or deny themselves the blessing of returning to a relationship with Him because they feel undeserving of God's gift of salvation.

Are you denying yourself the chance at a beautiful romance with our Christ because you feel undeserving? List the reasons why you feel undeserving of this relationship with Christ.

Read Romans 3:23 & 24

Now **write Romans 3:23** in your own words.

Who does the Bible say is deserving of salvation?

The truth is that none of us are deserving of salvation. But out of an intense love for us God sent His Son to lavishly pour out his grace on us by paying the ultimate price for us, so that we could one day be with Him in heaven despite our sins. It is up to us to accept this precious gift.

5.) The writer mentions thinking she had done all the good things in her life through her own power at one point.

Read 2 Corinthians 3:5.

This scripture clearly states that our competence comes from only one place: God.

List below the areas of your life over which you have assumed "control" and/or the things you have taken credit for when the glory really belongs to God.

Take a moment to pray over those areas of your life. Release control back over to God in all areas of your life and ask God for forgiveness for trying to steal His glory for yourself. Ask Him for a heart of humility full of confidence only in Him.

6.) Many times Christians are referred to as the bride of Christ. He has a romance with us. He is trying to woo us to Himself in order to share with us an intimate relationship and give us the treasures He has in store for us. What images come to mind when you think of a "great romance"? Write down how you think those can relate to our relationship with Jesus. *Example: He sweeps her off her feet. Just as Christ wants to sweep us off our feet and be exciting to us.*

Great Romance	Apply to Christ's Love

Now that you are thinking in a romantic frame of mind, read the book of Songs of Solomon (a.k.a. Song of Songs). Allow yourself to be drawn in by the romance of it. Put yourself in the shoes of the "beloved" and see Jesus as the "lover".

7.) In chapter 2 verse 14 of Song of Songs you see how the "lover" has to call his beloved from out of a rocky hiding place. He is beckoning with desperation for the one He sees as beautiful. We often find ourselves in rocky hiding places trying to hide from the One who calls us beautiful.

Do you see that you are beautiful to Jesus? He is desperately beckoning for you to come out of your hiding place and walk with Him. Let him shower you in His mercies and love.

8.) Maybe you don't feel like you're the one hiding. Maybe you feel like you are the one searching.

Re-read Song of Songs 3:1-2.

Here, it is talking about the beloved searching for her lover. Do you feel like you are searching for God but not finding Him? If so, write down the ways you are currently searching for God and what it is you are hoping to find.

Many times God is right in front of us and because He may not reveal Himself in the way we feel He should, we miss Him.

- **Examine your heart and state of mind** in hearing from God. Be willing to hear something other than just what you want to hear.
- **Make sure you are looking for Him in the right places.** You wouldn't go to a clothing store hoping to find a gallon of milk. So why would you look for God in places where you have never experienced His presence before? It only makes sense to go where God is known to be. We are not saying God won't show Himself except at certain places, but if you are having a hard time finding Him, start with the obvious. That could be church, amongst Christian friends or anywhere you can focus and be reminded of Him and His ability to be with you.
- **Search His word.** Make sure you are opening your Bible on a daily basis. It is so much easier for us to find time to pray and talk to God than to sit and read the scripture, but we can't expect to hear Him if we are the ones doing all the talking. Pray that as you read His word He will reveal to you what He needs you to hear and understand. The Bible is God breathed which means these are His words to us. He is talking to us and His words are very much alive.
- **Listen!** Listen to that tug on your heart that you've been shrugging off. Listen to that voice that tells you when something seems right or wrong. Listen, even when what you think you are hearing doesn't sound like what you were hoping He would say. Then take it a step further and **OBEY.**

9.) In closing, we encourage you to **read Hosea chapters 1-3** all in one sitting. It is an amazing story of love and betrayal and redemption. It is the story of God and His people above all else. Take a moment to pray before reading it—asking God to show you His mercy, love, forgiveness and greatness. Ask Him to show you how much He loves you. Try to put yourself in the place of Hosea's wife or Israel. Be ready with a pen to makes notes on what speaks to you.

NOTES:

GOD STILL WRITES THE ORDERS

My story begins at a very young age. I was raised in a Christian home and I just knew that Jesus was part of my life. At the age of 8 I knew enough to know that I needed to ask Jesus into my heart. I did and was baptized soon after. Growing up I was active in Sunday School, Training Union, Girls in Action and Bible Drill, so of course Bible knowledge increased. However, it wasn't until much later that my relationship with Jesus really grew.

Fast forward several years and I have a wonderful husband and 2 beautiful little girls. My husband, Glenn, is on active duty with the U.S. Navy. We had recently returned to the states after spending 2 ½ years in Japan. Glenn had completed his training to become an Aerospace Physiologist and was about to receive orders for his first duty assignment as a physiologist. He had been told that if he finished first in his class he could pick his duty station. We discussed the options and we decided Corpus Christie, Texas would be our choice. Glenn finished first in his class so we just knew we would be headed to Texas. But you know when those orders arrived they were sending us to Norfolk, Virginia! What a shock! When Glenn tried to question things, he was just told he made the wrong choice. Pack for Virginia.

There was a reason we didn't want to go to Virginia. We had been told that people in the Norfolk/Virginia Beach area just didn't like military members or their families. In fact, we shouldn't be surprised if they were rude or hostile. So we headed to Virginia with a pretty big chip on our shoulders. We just knew the Navy sent us because we didn't want to go. Those people in Norfolk and Virginia Beach actually turned out to be pretty nice people.

It didn't take us long to find a place to live and then we started scouting the area for a church. On our very first Sunday we visited a church that, from the street, looked just right. You know, not too big, not too small, neat and clean—just right. Unfortunately it wasn't just right so we kept looking. The next Sunday we visited another church—closer to home—but much larger. I have to admit I was a little intimidated. We went to a young adult class and wouldn't you know, it was full of Navy people as well as those Virginians, and they really seemed to like each other. We had the most exciting Sunday School teacher either of us had ever had the privilege of hearing. The preacher was dynamic! Our girls had a great time and wanted to come back. We had found our church.

Our Sunday School teacher was inspiring! She had both of us wanting to dig deeper into scripture. She wasn't satisfied with "Sunday School" answers. She wanted to know why you believed what you said you believed. She questioned and made us think about our answers. For the first time I truly began to grow as a Christian. My relationship with Jesus grew from just having a Savior to having someone who was Lord of my life. There was a peace in my heart that had been missing. Our pastor was also teaching us how to learn to trust God, and we could not get enough teaching. Praise God! He sent us to Virginia!

So, just how do you "find" the church God has for you? That is a great question and a question we would answer differently now than we would have at that time. I do believe we have matured and learned to ask a few more questions. In 1976 we were concerned with what was happening in preschool Sunday school and in the infant nursery. In 2008 we might not even visit the preschool facilities for quite some time. However, as parents our first questions were: Are our children happy? Are they safe? Are they being taught the truth? Once our children became teenagers it became crucial to know what was happening in the youth group. Is the youth group grounded in the word of God? We needed to meet the youth pastor and find out the dynamics and goals of the group. As important as those things are, there are other issues.

For us, finding a church always involved checking out a Bible study class. Were the class members friendly? Was the teacher knowledgeable and did he/she teach from the Bible? And of course we always wanted to know that the pastor preached and taught the truth according to God's holy word. How do you know that the word of God is being taught? Acts 17:11 says the Bereans "examined the scriptures to see if what Paul said was true." Likewise we have to examine the scriptures for ourselves.

I haven't mentioned the most important part of the process yet and that would be prayer! God is so good! He has promised that if we lack wisdom we should ask God who gives generously (James 1:5.) In Matthew 7:7, we are told to ask, seek, and knock and we will find the answer we search for. There is nothing that can take the place of prayer! To go forward with every component except prayer leaves you wide open for mistakes. I know because we traveled that path and made assumptions about joining a church and we never asked God. We learned a very painful lesson and had to change churches.

Our orders to Norfolk, Virginia, were only for 18 months and then there would be orders to another place. We had been in Virginia about a year when Glenn and I looked at each other and said, "The Navy did not send us to Norfolk—God did!! The Department of the Navy sent those orders and paid for a move, but only because God directed it. What a lesson for this Navy couple to learn! We could not blame the Navy for sending us any place. We now had to talk to God about every move.

From Norfolk, Virginia, we went to Havelock, North Carolina, home of Marine Corps Air Station Cherry Point. What a shock for a "city girl!" I couldn't believe it. There were 3 red lights in the whole town. (Did God really mean to send us here?) Since the town was so small, there weren't that many churches to choose from so it didn't take long to find a church home. What a transition, from great evangelistic preaching in Virginia, to incredible teaching from the pulpit in North Carolina. Our four years in Havelock were spent growing. Our family grew from 4 to 5, but even more importantly, our faith was growing day by day. We each discovered our spiritual gifts and began to use them. At that time I probably would not have used the terminology "finding my spiritual gift." I probably would have said I was "looking for my place of service." However you want to phrase it the question is, "How do you discover what God has gifted you to do?"

For me it involved trying different things—like working in the nursery, or teaching a children's class or even cleaning out storage closets—and then discovering what you have a passion for doing. It was working with children's Bible Drill that I discovered I have a passion for wanting people to grow in God's word. That discovery led right to teaching. I also discovered I am very happy cleaning anything (maybe because there is instant gratification.) Some might say that is the gift of service. You might discover the gift God has given you by asking your close Christian friends what personality traits they see in you that would indicate a specific gift.

In the past 15 years or so it seems that a new tool has been refined and is in use in many churches. That tool, of course, is the spiritual gifts profile. There are several profiles available but it is amazing that the end results are pretty close to the same. I personally think the tests are fun to take and they are a fabulous tool. Sometimes you might discover hidden talents and it might give you the confidence needed to try something new. For me the most important issue was discovering which gifts I scored low in. For instance, I scored rather poorly in the gifts of mercy and evangelism. Does that low score mean that I am not obligated to do those things? Absolutely not! It does mean I need to be aware of and work on those issues more than ever. Jesus said in Luke 6:36, "Be merciful just as your Father is merciful." In Matthew 28:19-20 Jesus also said to "go and make disciples." He did not qualify those commands with the words, "If you have been given the gift then do these things."

If you are a believer and you think you have not been given a gift, think again. Romans 12 and I Corinthians 12 teach us about some of the gifts and as believers we each have at least one gift. Romans 12 says that we are all members of the same body with different gifts. I Corinthians 12-14 says that our gifts are given for the common good of the church. I Corinthians 14:12 specifically says that we should "try to excel in gifts that build up the church."

For the next 25 years God moved us 6 more times, He just used the Secretary of the Navy to sign the orders. I know I have made this story sound like a fairy tale with no problems. Absolutely not true! We experienced financial problems and had to count every penny. We also learned to tithe. Did we make decisions without consulting God? I am sorry to say that we did. There were consequences as a result, but we learned valuable lessons and tried not to make the same mistakes too many times. We had little girls who were sick, had broken bones, and were scared to go to new schools. We cried every time we left a place! You know, mostly we cried because we were leaving friends made at church. (Now we can look back and know that we have friends on the east coast, the west coast, the Gulf coast and a few places in between.) It hurt when we were far away and had fathers pass away. It was all those times that we were reminded that we were never alone. "Be strong and courageous, do not tremble or be dismayed, for the Lord your God is with you wherever you go." Joshua 1:9.

The blessings we received from each duty station are too numerous to mention. The biggest blessings came when each of our girls made a profession of faith and were baptized. Sometimes God even blessed us by revealing to us the reason we were sent to a certain place. The people God placed in our paths just overwhelm us and we thank God for each of them.

Now I know someone may read this statement of faith and say, "Easy for them to know where God wanted them to be, but I don't have any military connections, who is going to write my orders?" I must be truthful and tell you that was my biggest fear when it came time to retire from the Navy! Who writes the orders now? What a Mighty God we serve—He can write orders without the Navy!

Glenn applied for several jobs and each of them in a different state. He applied for jobs in the education field and for jobs in the corporate/government field. We prayed fervently asking God for wisdom and seeking His direction. Then Glenn had an interview with a small college in northwest Georgia, a job he really thought he wanted. He wanted me to come with him and check out the town—give my opinion. I dropped Glenn off at the college and proceeded to "check out" the town. As the day progressed my heart got heavier and heavier. I couldn't say why. It was a beautiful town. Eventually I made my way back to pick up Glenn and he walked out to the car with a huge smile on his face. I decided not to say a word about my heavy heart. Glenn started to talk and I started to cry! Uncontrollable tears! I couldn't explain the tears except to say that my heart hurt. All Glenn said was, "I think God just answered our prayers." Needless to say we didn't go to northwest Georgia. There were other interviews and there just wasn't peace in both of our hearts to say yes, nothing as dramatic as that first interview though. I think God used that particular time in northwest Georgia to teach me that He did not need the Navy to write orders. What an answer to prayer! What a reminder to seek God first (Matthew 6:33.)

Glenn took a job with Oklahoma State University in Tulsa, Oklahoma. We both had a total peace about accepting that position. The funny thing is that God put us in Tulsa so Glenn would be in just the right place to hear a call to full-time ministry. Couldn't God make that call from any other place? Absolutely He could! However, we might not have been positioned to hear and respond positively. Tulsa would not be our last move. Now we find ourselves in Warner Robins, Georgia, where Glenn is on staff with a wonderful church and I have my little niche. We will be approaching a second retirement in the next 10-12 years, so is this where God will leave us? Only God knows! I just know that I can trust and He will direct.

> Trust in the Lord with all your heart,
> Lean not on your own understanding,
> but in all your ways acknowledge Him,
> and He will direct your paths.
> Proverbs 3:5-6

NOTES:

GOD STILL WRITES THE ORDERS
STUDY QUESTIONS

1. Patricia talks early on about growing in knowledge of Christ but not in relationship with Christ. List some of the characteristics someone growing in knowledge would exhibit and some characteristics someone growing in relationship would display. It is ok if some of the characteristics are the same.

Knowledge: Relationship:

Do you feel you are growing both in knowledge and relationship or just one of those areas?

While Biblical knowledge is a very important piece of the puzzle for the Christian wanting to grow, it is not what causes us to grow in Christ. If you have made a personal decision for Christ and have asked Him to reside within you as Lord and Savior of your life, then you can experience that "sweetness" the author described all the time. Our growth comes from having a personal relationship with Christ and that grows as we begin to relinquish control over to Him and trust Him in our daily lives. As our relationship grows so will our desire for knowledge of Him and His word. When both knowledge and relationship are being fed it is then that we are growing into the women God created us to be.

Read Psalms 34:8. Write here what it says:

If you have not tasted that sweetness before, then now is the time to do so. **Read Romans 10:9-13**. Write here the main idea of this passage:

If you confess Jesus as Lord and believe in your heart God raised Him from the dead you will be saved. You can know that sweetness in your own life no matter what your circumstances.

Take time to thank God for His gift of Salvation through his Son Jesus Christ and bask in the sweetness He wants to pour over you.

2. Trusting God in every aspect of our lives is not as easy at it may sound. Has God ever asked you to go somewhere undesirable or do something you absolutely did not want to do? If so what was/is it?

What are some of the blessings or consequences you have seen after obeying or disobeying Gods direction in your life?

As Christians we have the Captain of all Captains. He can and is willing to lead us through all of life's storms. You don't want to find yourself stuck in a boat out in the middle of the ocean with a Captain not able or willing to steer you through the storms that will undoubtedly come. What "Captain" are you allowing to determine the course of your life? Would your destination be determined by money, friends, social status, career advancement, family, and/or personal or public recognition? Remember that all "earthly" things can be taken away in a moment's notice. If that were to happen, to what or whom would you cling to stay afloat?

Learn to let God control all areas of your life now so that when the storms arise you can have confidence He will carry you through them.

3. Sometimes things look "just right" like the first church mentioned in this story, yet they just aren't right. We as humans like to base our decisions and directions off of what we see and what we think things should look like and so many times it doesn't make sense to us why God wouldn't lead us in that direction. Whether it is a relationship, career move, or a new church home, He leads us where He needs us. And where He needs us may not be in that perfect looking job opportunity or that beautiful active church. He may be moving you from one good thing to a different greater thing. You have to listen to be in touch with how the Holy Spirit is communicating with you and be willing to go when He says it is time to move on or start anew. It takes trust.

Are there any areas in your life in which you are basing your decisions on what looks right instead of the way you feel the Holy Spirit is leading you? If so list them and pray for clear direction in that area.

If you are involved in a local church, by what criteria did you chose it? (Or if you are in the process of finding one)

God's leading in the Spirit:
Disagree   Strongly Agree
0___/___/___/___/___5___/___/___/___/___10

The look of the people inside (age, economic status, race, etc):
Disagree   Strongly Agree
0___/___/___/___/___5___/___/___/___/___10

Type of music:
Disagree   Strongly Agree
0___/___/___/___/___5___/___/___/___/___10

Location:
Disagree Strongly Agree
0___/___/___/___/___5___/___/___/___/___10

Biblical teaching from the pulpit:
Disagree   Strongly Agree
0___/___/___/___/___5___/___/___/___/___10

Size of the church:
Disagree   Strongly Agree
0___/___/___/___/___5___/___/___/___/___10

Children/youth/other programs available:
Disagree   Strongly Agree
0___/___/___/___/___5___/___/___/___/___10

Ministry opportunities:
Disagree   Strongly Agree
0___/___/___/___/___5___/___/___/___/___10

Examine your ratings and pray to God to reveal areas where you have trusted your own understanding rather than His. Thank Him for ways He has led you into His will.

4. God sometimes asks us to leave what we are comfortable with (friends, family, home, etc . . .). This can be very difficult for us to accept because we want to believe that God wouldn't ask us to leave something or someone that makes us happy. Is God asking you to give up something you want to hold on to? Is He calling you to do something or go somewhere that may be uncomfortable? Write down what it is He is asking you to do.

Read 1Peter 4: 12&13. Write in your own words what it says:

We are not to consider it strange when we are asked to do something that may cause us pain or bring on trials. We will be overjoyed when His glory is revealed. We may not know why or how what He is asking us to do will bring Him glory, but if we obey, in time we will see His glory prevail.

5. What are some personal things you do to determine whether or not your decisions are lining up with the direction God wants you to go?

In Henry Blackaby's study, Experiencing God, he outlines 5 Biblically based ways to determine if you are recognizing God's will in your life. Blackaby says that you must understand that God speaks through the following:

The Holy Spirit	(1Cor 2:9-16; John 14:26 & 16:12-15)
The Bible	(Hebrews 4:12 and Ephesians 6:17-18)
Prayer	(Romans 8:26-7; Jer 29:11-13; Ps 91:14-15)
Circumstances	(John 6:1-15 & Luke 7:11-17, for examples)
The Church	(Eph 4:15-16; Heb 10:25)

After reading Blackaby's work, it is impressed upon our hearts that the only way we are able to recognize God speaking in these ways is to maintain a close personal relationship with Him. If we have taken to only listening to the preacher rather than examining the Word of God for ourselves, or rely on what others say alone because we see them as "godly", then we are out of the will of God and will most likely not hear Him when He speaks. We cannot rely on others to maintain a relationship with Christ for us. We must invest the time, effort and heart it takes to maintain that relationship for ourselves. Do we have relationships that are truly intimate if we rely on a third party to relay information between us?

Let's take a look at each element more closely . . .

A.) If we are to hear God speaking to us through the Holy Spirit, what must first be true in our lives?

When the Holy Spirit speaks to you—what is the usual method of communication? This may be different for each person. Describe here a time when you clearly heard the Holy Spirit speaking to you.

B.) If we are to hear God speak to us through the Bible, what must first be true in our lives?

When God speaks to you through the Bible, how do you know? Describe a time when it was clear God used His Work to speak directly to your specific circumstances.

C.) If God is going to speak to you through prayer, what first must be true in your life?

When God speaks to you through prayer, how do you respond? Describe a time when you heard God speaking through prayer. How did you respond?

C.) If God is going to speak to you through circumstances, what must first be true in your life if you are to understand Him?

Describe a time when you knew God was using the circumstances in your life to speak His direction/comfort/love to you.

D.) **Read John 6:1-15**. Do you think the disciples understood what was happening at the time? Explain :

If God is going to speak to you through other believers, what things must first be true in your life for you to recognize His voice in them?

Describe a time in your life when God clearly spoke to you through another believer. How did you respond?

If you are having trouble answering these questions, we implore you to go to God right now, repent of any sin, declare your desire to hear Him and then start doing those things that you need to do in order to walk closely with the Lord Jesus. First of all, you must have the gift of the Holy Spirit through the salvation of Jesus Christ to be able to hear Him. Then, for example, begin spending time devoted to studying God's word. Spend time each day in prayer. Begin examining the circumstances of your life to search for God's hand and adjust your attitude to accept His instruction. If you are not currently involved in a local church body of believers, seek one out under God's direction through prayer. If you do attend a local church, but find that you aren't "fulfilled" examine the reasons why . . . have you gotten personally involved in some ministry at the church? Have you made an effort to make friends? To be involved in Bible study groups? Is the teaching from the pulpit Biblical?

6. **Read Proverbs 3: 5&6.**

These verses are some of the most commonly quoted scriptures and yet when we are having difficulty "letting go and letting God" we are led to these verses and they refresh our mind as if it were the first time we had ever heard them.

Let's take a closer look and really study this passage:

> Trust in the Lord with all your heart
> Lean not on your own understanding
> In all your ways acknowledge Him
> And He will direct your paths.

First, **write it out** for yourself, contemplating in your heart the meaning of these words.

Now, **say it aloud** to yourself, listening carefully to the message contained within.

Go to the verse and circle any words that particularly stand out to you—especially the "**action**" words.

Now in your own words, **summarize** what the Holy Spirit is saying to you in this passage.

Now, if at all possible, go to the notes in a study Bible and review what the notes say regarding this passage. Also, note any other scripture passages that are referred to in the margin by this passage. Chose two of those passages to read to gain insight and context within the scope of the Bible.

(If you don't have a study Bible, the internet can be a great resource—www.biblegateway.com and the biblescope app for iPhone are a couple of good examples. There are also plenty of free bibles for e-readers.)

Write here what additional insights you gained or information you learned by expanding your study in this manner:

Next, we challenge you to memorize this
passage and spend time contemplating it each day for the next week.
Remember index cards and sticky notes around the house can be very helpful!

WHY NOT ME?

Why not me? Those are the words I thought at age 29 while lying in a hospital bed five months pregnant. After not feeling well I had finally found out why. The x-rays and scans showed a two and a half inch mass in my right lung. The doctor that came to me with this news also told me that he'd never seen a mass of such a large size that wasn't cancerous.

I'd always had an easy life with few struggles or tragedies. So I figured why not me? Bad things happen all of the time and it just happens to be my time.

Everything was so uncertain. We didn't know what kind of cancer I had or if I or the baby would survive it. The only thing that was certain is just how great our God is. Second Samuel 7:22 says it perfectly. "How great you are, O Sovereign LORD! There is no one like you, and there is no God but you, as we have heard with our own ears." I quickly realized that this problem was way too big for me. While waiting in the hospital for a week and a half for the results of tests and procedures God gave me the opportunity to really spend some quality time with Him. I took God up on His offer and read His Word, prayed and waited. God surrounded me in His presence during that time. He placed me in a hospital that proclaimed His Name and gave me an unbelievable support system through my family, friends and fellow believers. I had never seen how powerful the body of Christ could be. Christians all over the world lifted up prayers for me and my family.

We still weren't sure as to what kind of cancer I had but the doctors thought my best chance for survival was to remove my right lung. I thought this was a great idea. After all, I had a wonderful husband, two beautiful girls and another baby on the way and I wanted what was best to survive.

The evening before the surgery, God moved some mountains for us. Some church leaders in the community came and anointed me and later on an acquaintance and his wife came and did the same thing. I believe through the power of prayer and obedience on their part God gave us a miracle. James 5:14-16 says "Is any one of you sick? He should call to the elders of the church to pray over him and anoint him with oil in the name of the Lord and the prayer offered in faith will make the sick person well; the Lord will raise him up. If he has sinned he will be forgiven. Therefore confess your sins to each other and pray for each other so that you may be healed. The prayer of a righteous man is powerful and effective." The next morning God showed me He had something better for me than removing my lung. I was officially diagnosed with choriocarcinoma. It is a very rare type of cancer but it is also considered curable.

Along with the good news also came some bad. My doctor told me I was going to have to abort the baby for the sake of my life. This news was very upsetting. Immediately after telling me this news the doctor saw how upset I was and made a phone call to an expert in the field. It was decided that I would carry the baby through the rigorous chemotherapy regimen and hopefully everything would be okay for me and the baby. After a couple of months of chemo God showed us another miracle. Our healthy baby girl was delivered eight weeks early.

About the time I thought things were going well with my health we found out I had a brain tumor that needed to be removed immediately. It was only two weeks after having our little girl that I was back in the hospital undergoing brain surgery. This was the scariest time for me because I really feared not being able to be alive to be a wife for my husband and a mother to my children. I knew that God's will was the place to be whether by life or by death but the idea of not fulfilling my dreams of wife and Mommy terrified me. I think about Job when he said in Job 1:21b "The LORD gave and the LORD has taken away; may the name of the LORD be praised" and remember that everything is about God's glory not about the circumstance of the moment. The surgery was a great success and I began receiving my final rounds of chemo.

This whole process started while on vacation in Florida. We lived in FL for a half a year until I was finished with my cancer treatments. I was so excited to come home and sink back into my normal life. Sink was about all I did. I had a hard time adjusting to being mommy again. Just dealing with the daily activities of three children under the age of four was difficult. I had plenty of help taking care of things but the emotional and mental help is what I lacked. Somewhere in the midst of all the miracles and blessings I had taken my focus off of God and placed it on myself. It occurred to me that I was so quick to turn the "big" things over to God but what He really wants is for me to turn it all over to Him. He wants me to have that God can move mountains trust in Him all of the time not just for those things that I have labeled big.

As I think back on that year I shouldn't only think of the bad circumstances as "why not me?" circumstances. It was an amazing year and God used so many people to make a positive impact in my life and for the kingdom of God. He showed Himself to me in such a powerful way that I need to be asking God to allow me to be a vessel for His glory and say to Him "why not me?"

Notes:

WHY NOT ME?
STUDY QUESTIONS

1. If you had to assess your life based on the struggles you have faced, what rating would it have?

0 ——————————————————— 5 ——————————————————— 10

Little Struggle   Tremendous Struggle

If given a diagnosis like the one given to Kim or if faced with a struggle you would consider to be tremendous, what do you imagine your reaction would be like? Would your reaction be more like Kim's, "Why not me?" or would you be prone to ask "why me?"

2. Kim and her husband chose to react to this uncertain and frightening time by going to God rather than succumbing to the despair that naturally accompanies this type of event. It has been said that the true test of faith and our true witness is proved and seen during times of crisis such as these. What did Kim's attitude and choice to rely on God say to those around her?

As Christians we are always being watched to see how we will handle different situations. People want to see if we will react differently than those without the Hope of Christ. Think over some of your recent reactions to different circumstances. Would those in view of you see a reflection of Christ in your actions and attitude?

List your reasoning for your answer.

Philippians 1:27 says, *"Whatever happens, conduct yourself in a manner worthy of the Gospel of Christ."* If we conducted ourselves in this manner in every circumstance or trial, facing them would become a different experience and an opportunity for spiritual growth, not only for ourselves but for those in view of us.

3. **Read John 9:1-7.** The Disciples thought the man was blind due to his own or his parents' sin, but why did Jesus say the man was blind? (vs.3)

Though sometimes illness is the result of our own sin or that of our parents, we must remember that we can be healed by the power of Jesus Christ. Nothing is too big for Him to handle. Not our worst sin, not the most trying circumstances and most assuredly not even cancer.

Read Mark 2:1-12.

Write down the first thing Jesus said to the paralyzed man.

Which did Jesus do first, forgive the man's sin or heal the paralyzed man's body?

It was not until the religious leaders rose in anger at the presumption Jesus made with that act that Jesus divinely healed the man's physical sickness. Through this God was glorified and Jesus' power to forgive sin was confirmed. It is obvious through this story that, to Jesus, the need for healing the sickness of our hearts (sin) is more important to Him than the healing of our physical bodies. In either case, whether in healing of our sins through forgiveness or through healing of our bodies, our main concern should be that God receive the glory and that we allow Him to use us as He sees fit to be the vessels in which He uses to further His kingdom.

One of the most effective messengers of God's Word was Paul, a celebrated man of faith whose writings compose over half of the New Testament. Read 2 Corinthians 12:7-10. It is never indicated in scripture what Paul's thorn was. It could have been anything from a physical disability, to disease, to depression, to temptation. Whatever it was, Paul pleaded with God to remove it. How many times did Paul plead to the Lord for deliverance from his "thorn"?

What was God's response to him?

How did Paul then choose to view this thorn?

Are you, like Paul, ready to give God the glory in your life even if physical healing or the removal of whatever your thorn may be is not in God's plan?

4. There is no doubt Kim and her husband drew their strength from the Almighty. Through personal Bible study and time with God they were able to store up strength for this time in which they would need strength beyond themselves. They had stored up what we will call "spiritual currency." How much spiritual currency do you have stored up? Are you making daily deposits into your spiritual account? Spiritual currency is presented to us as those things we do that bring us closer to God—the relationship we build with Him not only in difficult times but also in prosperous times.

What are some ways in which you are currently building up spiritual currency in your own life?

If you haven't put the spiritual currency in your bank, you will have nothing on which to draw during those periods of famine and strife. Make a conscious effort to invest more in your spiritual bank than in your monetary one. **Look up Mathew 6:19&20**. Fill in the blanks below.

"Do not store up for yourselves _____ ____ _____, where moth and rust destroy, and where thieves break in and steal. But store up for yourselves _____ ____ _____, where moth and rust do not destroy, and where thieves do not break in and steal. For where your _____ is, there your _____ will be also."

5. God's word promises those of us who are Christians that we will one day live a life with no pain, sorrow, or stress. We will one day be completely made perfect. Look up the following verses and write down what they have to say about the promises God gives us about our future.

2 Corinthians 5:1

John 14:1—3
Revelation 21:3-4

We have descriptions throughout the Bible that reference a little of what we can expect in Heaven. Streets of gold, gates of pearls, etc . . . Now take a moment and visualize what you believe Heaven will be like. Write down what you see and the things you are most looking forward to. When you are done take a moment and thank God for your secured place there with Him one day. Live a life of confidence, full of hope, knowing that this is the prize in which we will have when our temporary home passes away and our eternity with the Father begins. (If you would like more information and specific references to Bible passages on heaven—Randy Alcorn's book Heaven is a great resource.)

PERFECTING THE TAPESTRY

All of my life I have been drawn to the rich colors and texture of tapestry. Twenty something years ago a dear friend, who knew of my admiration, gave me a framed piece of tapestry with the following poem. I have always sensed it was a spiritual compass for my life:

The Weaver
by Benjamin Malacia Franklin
(Originally titled, "Just a Weaver")

My life is just a weaving
Between my Lord and me.
I cannot change the color
For He works most steadily.

Oft times He weaves the sorrow
And I in foolish pride
Forget He sees the upper
And I the underside.

Until the loom is silent
And the shuttle cease to fly,
Will God roll back the canvas
And explain the reason why.

The dark threads are as needful
In the skillful Weaver's Hand
As the golden threads of silver
He has patterned in His Plan.

Our relationship had started out so perfectly. He was smart, funny, highly respected, educated, romantic, spiritual, a great Bible teacher and he was even tall! (I am 5'9".) My husband appeared to be the man of my dreams after coming out of relationships with men who had been wounded, were emotionally unavailable and didn't genuinely like me for who I was. I did realize though that love can be blind, so I prayed a very specific prayer: "Lord, don't let me marry this man if it will not make me a better Christian." God honored that prayer, but in a way I hadn't intended . . .

That August day my life changed forever, as I watched my husband and two children drive down the driveway to visit his out of state relatives and for him to work on some of his research. I call it the day I got "hit by the bus". As they drove away I prayed a prayer of thanksgiving to God for giving me such a wonderful husband and family. Then I went to do some work on the new computer my husband had begged me to get. I looked forward to some quiet time to work on an important professional presentation I was going to do. As I sat there I felt like God was physically holding the sides of my face and saying, "It is time for you to know something". At that time I had almost no computer knowledge. How I was able to find and see what I did, I couldn't tell you.

When I first saw the vile pornographic pages that my husband had visited, I momentarily went into denial, but it was short-lived. The evidence piled up. I had to face the reality that the man who was a respected church and community leader had another side to his life. I would have bet the lives of my children that my husband was not capable of doing the things I would later find he had done. I had never seen him really even look at another woman. It did not fit with anything I had ever seen him do or say. How could this be the same man I had met in 1987?

Initially I thought the injuries were severe, but knew I had a high pain tolerance. When I considered losing my marriage and all my hopes and dreams for the future and my two small children's future, I was willing to forgive, pay the price, endure the pain and do the work it would take to recover. We went to counseling where my husband was quickly identified as an SA (sex addict) and had been since boyhood. I, of course, was the co-dependent. As with all good codependents, I immediately went into emergency management mode to "control" and 'fix' the problem and do damage control. In a strange way I was "relieved" to finally be able to identify the nameless, invisible battle I had sensed for years.

It wasn't long into the marriage before I sensed that his family and work and even his entertainment were much more important than I was to him. Quickly he even lost much interest in me sexually, though I was in my physical prime. I knew if I made him choose I would have to face the reality of his choices. If I ever broached the subject, he would quickly tell me I was selfish, controlling or just being jealous. He quickly learned that if he attacked my character, especially with a "spiritual twist" he could get me to apologize and take the blame for the conflict. I remember one stormy night he was hours later than he told me he would be. I sensed something was "wrong". I was sick with worry, fearing I had lost the love of my life. When he finally came home I broke down and sobbed. He curtly told me I was being ridiculous. Something changed in me that night: I started to numb out my intense feelings that were apparently ridiculous.

So I modified my expectations and my dreams and chose to see the good in him and in our marriage. I was proud to be his wife and felt important when I was with him. I chose to trust him when he was away from me, traveling with others for his job. People continued to tell me how lucky I was to have such an awesome godly husband. I frequently quoted 1 Corinthians13:4-8

(NASB) to myself, reminding myself that "Love is patient, kind, NOT jealous . . . . does not seek its own, is not provoked or take into account wrongs suffered . . . Love bears all things, believes all things, hopes all things, endures all things" and in the (NIV) version vs. 7 says "it always protects, always trusts, always hopes and always perseveres!" This is the kind of godly wife and woman I wanted to be. So I chose to be thankful for what I had and make the most of it. Overall, I considered our marriage one of the best around and so did everyone else. My husband always treated me honorably in public and was fairly supportive of my accomplishments. He always voiced a respectful attitude toward women. Many people sought his counsel. Besides, we had lots of fun times together!

In 1993 the birth of my son changed me profoundly. That instant, the overwhelming love I had for that child in my arms helped me get a glimmer of how God loved me as his child. That first Sunday as I held my precious son during the communion service I was deeply moved. For the first time in my life I realized the enormity of John 3:16. I served a God who loved me so much that he would give up the thing that would cost him the most! That he would give up his only Son for me! As a new mother I couldn't imagine giving up my precious baby for anyone, much less ungrateful sinners.

During the actual birth of my son, I felt more loved and appreciated by my husband than at any other time in our marriage. I hoped that having a family of our own would help him get a better perspective on what was truly important. Again I had to grieve that he didn't keep his promise to stop traveling once we started a family. Again I chose to see the good and revel in it. I focused my emotional energy on the joys of being a mother.

Then in June of 1995, as a quiet sadness filled the hospital room, we lost our Sarah Grace. I held my newborn daughter as her heart slowly ceased to beat, releasing her back to the God who had given her to me for such a brief period.

In the next weeks and months I slowly processed through my grief and mixed emotions. Finally I got to what I called the "love phase". I felt an unfamiliar closeness with God, with a deep knowing that he was walking through this with me. He hadn't abandoned me and he wasn't punishing me. Instead he was lovingly providing all my needs, including real friends, family, scripture and even books that spoke to my heart.

In that dark valley I also came to understand that no other human could fully understand exactly what I was feeling or needed in any given moment. I had anticipated following my husband's lead through the grief process, but he seemed to be stuck in the "angry phase." I found myself grieving alone, fearful of pushing my husband away from God. Yet, I felt God grieved with me and gave me a strength I knew was not from within me. He even made me more compassionate, appreciative and useful in His Kingdom through this experience. I had become vulnerable and thus much more approachable. I had also learned not to judge how others grieve or deal with a difficult situation. Eventually the excruciating grief changed to a warm place in my heart that treasured this little girl I had waiting on me in heaven and for eternity.

One day I stood on my back deck and felt a sense of relief. I said to myself "I have survived this tragedy and there is hope for happiness again . . . . this was almost too easy". Almost immediately I heard a distinct strong voice in my spirit saying, "This was to prepare you for something much bigger." WHAT! I mustered all the spiritual grit I could and said, "Yes, Lord". I could relate to the apostle Peter when he responded to Jesus who asked his disciples if they wanted to leave him too. John 6:68 "Lord, to whom shall we go? You have the words of eternal life. We believe and know that you are the Holy One of God". I knew God had supernaturally provided for me in this valley and he would provide for me no matter what. I also had a bolstered and exaggerated confidence in my ability to "be strong" in the difficult times. Like Peter, I would also crumble under pressure, but eventually run back to the arms of my Savior with renewed zeal and passion. I was not prepared for the "loss" God would allow in my life over the next few years. It came from the last place I could imagine, the place where I had no defenses . . . and it took me to the very dark and dangerous edge.

The dark, deep and painful valley God would allow me to go through in the next few years was, as Dr. Dobson would say, "tough love". He knew the beautiful and intricate tapestry he had designed for his child to be. He also knew what it would take to get me to give up the bland, predictable and minimally useful little piece of plaid I was clutching. He loved me enough to forcefully extract the threads of my tapestry that distorted the image he wanted to create. He helped me pull out the various idols, the pride, the religious heritage and other things that kept me from being totally reliant on him. He would lovingly and painstakingly reveal the "lies" and the "arrows" and the "false lovers" woven in by Satan to keep me from being the masterpiece God intended for me to be. He wisely required that I help identify and extract some of these false fibers. I am still on the loom. How much easier it is to remove the damaged threads before they have become entwined with others. I believe God uses the Holy Spirit to enlighten and convict me. He is a gentleman and he never forces me to comply with the divine design. I am slowly learning to trust that he sees the big picture in light of eternity, even when all I can see is the pain and the mess of the moment.

And that brings us back to the day I was hit by that bus. After my husband was identified as a sex addict, I immediately went into godly "forgiveness" mode and even started confessing every sin I could think of to show my husband I didn't think I was perfect. Later my counselor encouraged me to listen to the Holy Spirit's timing for forgiveness. She helped me see that perhaps I was offering rather 'cheap' forgiveness. It much easier to "forgive and forget" than to really face the pain and really tally the cost of the loss. I was convinced that my sweet and wonderful husband was not like the other guys I heard about. I didn't see my husband as a typical "addict"; instead I believed and stated, "He is a great guy with a problem." Now that we understood "the problem" we would have an awesome marriage. He would stop seeing himself as the "victim" and me as the "bad guy". He would finally be able to see me for who I was and love me. Of course he would always be grateful for the forgiveness extended to him. Satan had attacked our marriage, but we were going to victoriously bring glory to God! That was my plan!

Almost immediately we had access to the top experts in the field of SA. I gratefully recognized that we had amazing resources (counselors, groups, books, retreats, workshops and the finances to participate) that few others had. I knew it was from God, but I didn't fully understand "why". In my typical Pollyanna style I claimed victory over this battle, confident that we would become the poster-couple for SA in the Christian community. We would show others how to save their marriages. (No one told me that only about 2% of SA marriages survive.)

As with most couples dealing with SA, we went through a glorious "honeymoon" phase. We were both relieved that the secret was out and our life was still pretty much intact. None of our family or community knew any different. He told me the things I wanted and needed to hear.

For a brief period we reveled in our heightened physical and emotional connection. I was willing to forgive an entire marriage of lies and deceit, as well as infidelity of the heart, mind and body. I was willing to forgive the huge amount of money he had used for his addiction. I even chose to put off dealing with the risk of having an STD for the time being. However, I could not and would not allow him to participate in any of his sinful behaviors and remain married to me. I felt convicted that this was God's standard and I didn't have the right to dilute it. Even though I was very beat up by many well-meaning Christians who thought I should continue to tolerate it since it was labeled "an addiction".

Soon the honeymoon was over. Counselors helped me see that the problem was not just the behaviors, but it was an entire addictive personality, which is selfish, deceitful and not willing to take responsibility. He continued to lie to me. I was devastated and felt I couldn't handle any more lies! He continued to take comfort in the things he hadn't done. I learned that addicts usually see themselves as the victims . . . and the heroes. They usually minimize their behavior and blame others. My husband felt that he had gotten caught . . . had said, "I am sorry" . . . . that should be the end of it. If we still had any problems it was because I had "issues" or because I wasn't willing to forgive him. The experts helped me understand that an SA takes 5-7 yrs of active recovery and accountability to 'thaw out" and to start realizing the harm they have caused. I committed to God that I would wait as long as it took if there was no infidelity. Though I had the right to a scriptural divorce at that time, I felt that God was asking me to surrender that trump card, and stop relying on it as my "back-up plan." God wanted me to trust Him to protect me.

Going through counseling was tumultuous and "crazy making". Even the best of counselors occasionally get "hooked" by an addict's charm and "victim" cries. Many times I felt like a woman who was lying beaten and battered in her own blood, having just been brutally raped. Instead of compassion and help I often felt the rapist and others were standing over me criticizing me, implying I got what I deserved. After all, the rapist couldn't help himself . . . . he is an addict. The truth of one counselor's words would come back to me over and over. She said, "An addict will say or do whatever they need to say or do to get out of the pain of the moment. As soon as they say it . . . they BELIEVE it is true. The louder they say it the more they believe it." An addict is not living in reality. Truth has no bearing on anything. An addict is not interested in understanding, only in proving they are the victims and what happened wasn't their fault.

There were some brief periods early on when my husband had some clarity about his problem and what he had done. Unfortunately recovery and repentance never 'stuck'. The more I understood about his childhood traumas the more compassionate I was. However I finally realized going in the cage with a wounded tiger was only getting me cut to shreds. He was not and is still not capable of seeing my heart or intent. I finally learned to leave that to the experts. I finally came to the conclusion that I was insane if I continued to try to do couples counseling with an addict who wasn't consistently working on his stuff. Our counselor warned us that a relationship would not work if both people were not committed to doing their own recovery. Things continued to worsen.

The next year was an emotional roller coaster for me. An addict like my husband was able to pull off his 'double life' so flawlessly, because he has mastered the art of compartmentalizing his sin. It was like Dr Jekyll and Mr. Hyde. Prior to the day I got "hit by the bus" I had not seen these visible personality changes or the overt verbal abuse. One day he would write the most tender loving words in a card, the next day he would blame me for all our marriage issues . . . and coldly say "It didn't have to be this way . . . if you would have only . . ." God continued to provide for me with both individual and group Christian counseling. I wanted and needed to thoroughly deal with my issues. A wise counselor had told me: "whatever you don't work through, you will pass on to your children". My children deserved a whole and healthy mom. It took me a couple of years to realize I didn't cause his addiction and I couldn't fix it. All I could do was deal with my own issues and see why I had been drawn to someone who would treat me this way . . . or I was bound to stay in the sickness or repeat it. As I progressed though counseling I started to really deal with what I had lost, and to grieve what my husband's addiction had cost me.

Like the frog in the heating water I slowly tolerated more and more humiliation and abuse. Ironically he pulled away more and more and started telling me I should be like the "other women". I was desperate to hold on to him, I couldn't bear losing him. If he left me it would mean I was truly unlovable. Who was I without him? If I couldn't keep this marriage together I would be failing God. His verbal abuse escalated until, on more than one occasion, I became very suicidal in my thoughts. For the first time in my life I understood suicide. At times my pain and despair were so severe I was incapable of caring, even about my precious children. When pain is that intense and you see no relief in sight, you feel you cannot go on. One day I came dangerously close to following through with my suicidal thoughts. I know it was God who gave me a picture in my mind of my young son sadly saying "why mommy?" It was the picture I needed to live another day. I understood why people cut themselves; any sensation is better than the emotional torture. I understood why people go off into their own mental world to escape the abuse. I would go out and lay on the cold wet driveway to feel something other than the pain, which my husband then used as emotional ammunition to paint me as crazy or "the problem". One day I truly felt I was unable to go on breathing; I just didn't have the strength. I had finally reached my "bottom". I came to the humble realization that I was NOT strong. I had nothing left. If God didn't help me breathe, I couldn't go on. I was totally and utterly dependent on him. FINALLY! What a relief to know I didn't have to be strong; I just had to continue to turn to God as my source.

I felt God was carrying me over the dark abyss; he helped me understand something. He was firmly grasping my arms with his strong hands and he wasn't going to drop me! I could choose to look up into his loving face and listen to his voice of truth . . . or I could choose to look down in the scary abyss and "listen" to the lies and the screams that tried to convince me I was doomed. I could even choose to pull away from his loving arms. I repeatedly pleaded with God not to let my pain be in vain. Later I would see the amazing ways he honored that request. I asked God to mold me into a grace-filled woman able to help others along the journey.

One day after hearing yet another lie, I started to spiral down in despair. My recent counseling had helped me see the truth; that I only start spiraling down when I allowed him to verbally abuse me. He said: "do you want me to leave". (My husband had always threatened me that if I ever kicked him out and others found out, the marriage would be over.) God gave me the courage to say, "Yes, I do want you to leave". From that moment I started to regain my sanity and clarity. That night I cried for joy because of the peace and safety I felt. I went to sleep feeling like I was sleeping in the strong loving arms of my spiritual husband, Jesus. I had always known Jesus was God's precious Son who had obediently died for my sins so that I could spend eternity with him and his Father forever. But it was at this point in my life I started to understand the awe of having him as my ever-faithful bridegroom. He thought of me when he was being beaten and crucified. He was not only being obedient to his Father, he lovingly and willingly paid the ransom, the costly bride price. I stood naked and degraded, but he has called me by name to be his. He has gone to prepare for the wedding and the eternal honeymoon. He thinks I am worth it! This is better than any romance novel or movie . . . and it is true!!!

For the next couple of years I continued to 'wait' from a safe distance. For the most part I had learned to believe behavior . . . NOT words. But, more times than I care to admit, I would fall for the "charm", and begin to hope again that he was really starting to change. I now understand the statistic about abused women leaving 6-9 times before they finally leave for good. God was so patient with me and would gently say to me, "If you need to hit your head against that wall one more time to see that it is still hard, go ahead." However, God loved me dearly and would almost immediately reveal the very things that I needed to see, as I needed to see them. My husband was quite happy in his new 'almost single" lifestyle. He felt entitled to break all the 'rules' he had agreed to and returned to the same playground, same friends and lied about his whereabouts. His flirting was much more obvious in the community. This man had continued to spiritually spiral down, yet continued to skillfully live a double life going to church with his friends and being the applauded hero at work. His own family even considered him to be the victim. Multiple times he asked me "why don't you just divorce me?" This would allow him to firmly establish his victim-hood.

Seeing his continued spiritual decline and complete lack of remorse, I finally pleaded with God: "Lord, you know I made a covenant to you to wait as long as it takes. But Lord, if this man is not going to ever change would YOU please release me!" Shortly after that my husband who had once preached strongly against divorce now said it was "God's will" and filed for divorce. In 2003, 3 ½ yrs after I got "hit by the bus" I was legally, morally, emotionally and financially set free. God gave me a guilt-free divorce. I would never have to look back and wonder if I tried hard enough or waited long enough. I was granted primary custody of my children, allowing me to protect them, without ever having to go to court. In spite of my fears, God has taken care of all of my needs, beyond what I could have imagined.

Yes, I still grieve the choices my ex-husband made and the consequences of his sin. I deplore the label "divorced" and the shame and awkwardness that comes with it. Occasionally I still have moments of intense sadness and loneliness, especially when others are celebrating "couples events" or family events. I grieve for my children; there will always be the awkwardness of having divorced parents . . . every special occasion will be tainted. The cost of sin is very high. The TRUTH is that all these feelings of grief and loss are normal God given emotions. Someone described divorce as the tearing apart of two pieces of paper that were glued together, both pieces of paper are permanently damaged to some degree.

I am still in "recovery" according to the definition I have adopted: becoming the person God uniquely created me to be. Apparently it was not God's plan that I help the 2% of the women whose marriages survive SA, but rather be a resource and support for the 98% that don't. The trials and losses have caused me to be less judgmental and critical. I am privileged to have opportunities to help others who are in the midst of their storm . . . to hear the voice of truth rather than the lies. I grieve to think of how I harmed people back before my trials . . . when I knew it all. Ironically God has used me, in my brokenness, exceedingly more than when my life seemed neat and orderly.

As the apostle Paul says "when I am weak, then am I strong". I am a work of art still very much on the loom, trying to cooperate with the Master Weaver. Amazingly I can see that he has even turned some of my mistakes into part of the pattern. I am not completed, but praise God I am not the same person who started out the journey!

Stepping back from the tapestry I am able to get a hint of the multi—dimensional beauty my master is creating; beauty, depth and perspective that could only come with the deep dark rich colors of rejection, sorrow and loss. They create beautiful contrast next to the bright and shimmering threads.

In Secrets of the Vine, Bruce Wilkerson describes a biblical principle about the trials of the painful pruning process that I have found true in my life. Sometimes God prunes me because of willful sin or maybe even unrealized sin (such as my idolatry). Therefore, when trials come my way I need to always start with some soul searching and ask God to show me if there is any sin in my life. Other times he prunes off of me some of my earthly treasures and delights that I have allowed become distractions so I can focus on my purpose, and bear some eternal fruit. Thirdly, as I grow in the Lord he prunes me severely when he wants to give me the "opportunity to bear much fruit." The final type of pruning seems to sever the things and relationships I think I can't live without. A vineyard will not yield a great harvest without aggressive pruning. God's pruning is not meant to harm me, but to help me to fulfill my God-given purpose. Faith isn't faith until it is tested. It is when we can't understand or see and still choose to believe that the sovereign God of the universe has a plan. His role for us is so much bigger than the small roles we script for ourselves. His plan is to bless us in view of eternity. In reality not all trials can be 'explained". Some trials and losses will not be understood until we step into eternity in the presence of the Master Weaver and see the full beauty of the tapestry in its entirety as woven by our all knowing and all loving God.

PERFECTING THE TAPESTRY
STUDY QUESTIONS

1. Have you ever been the one standing in front of the bus? Has your life ever been seemingly going fine when the bottom fell out and life was suddenly never going to be the same?

Take a moment to describe this crisis and how your life was forever changed.

In order for us to recognize the Holy Spirit drawing us to things we need to know, we must first be able to recognize the Spirit. Just as Carol knew He was drawing her to something on the computer she needed to know, we too must be in close enough fellowship with Him to realize when He is trying to reveal something to us.

2. What types of losses would occur when finding out one's spouse has been unfaithful?

Define the term adultery in your own words:

What dangers lie with the act of adultery?

The Bible gives us much on the topic of how God views faithfulness. Proverbs is a particularly rich book for learning the wisdom of righteous living. **Read Proverbs 5 or 6:20-29 or Proverbs 7**. List out the pearls of wisdom that particularly strike you as poignant and relevant: {For example: Proverbs 7:21 tells us that we are seduced with smooth talk—we aren't looking at the sin with realistic eyes—we never see it as dirty and harmful as it truly is when we delve into it. Proverbs

7:3 tells us to bind the teachings on our hearts and fingers—having them written in our hearts will help us in that time of temptation to draw from their strength.}

The 10 Commandments listed in Deuteronomy 5 tell us not to commit adultery and not to covet our neighbor's wife or belongings. Jesus then takes it to another level and tells us in Luke 16:18 that anyone who divorces his wife (*except for infidelity*) and marries another woman commits adultery, and the man who marries a divorced woman commits adultery. (see also Matt 19:9) And yet that is not as far as he takes it. In Matthew 5:27-28, Jesus states, "You have heard that it was said, 'Do not commit adultery.' But I tell you that anyone who looks at a woman lustfully has already committed adultery with her in his heart."

In your view, is the level of betrayal any different when the errant relationship exists only in cyberspace?

How is it the same as a physical betrayal and how is it different?

Does God make a distinction, based on the previous verses?

List other ways a spouse can be betrayed:

3. After experiencing such a betrayal, we are all faced with the issue of forgiveness. We know that the Bible calls us to forgive those who have wounded us, but that process can be over-whelming. Sometimes we offer up what the writer calls "cheap forgiveness" in order to skip to the end of the process in hopes of avoiding much of the pain. The problem with this is that neither party is able to experience the true healing that comes only by walking through the pain associated with confronting the betrayal.

Have you ever offered up cheap forgiveness or had it offered to you? Describe:

What were the effects to your relationship with that person as a result of such forgiveness?

4. Read Luke 11:39-54.

What was Jesus' attitude toward the Pharisees?

As a result of this exchange between Jesus and the Pharisees, Jesus' life becomes more difficult. They were incensed by Jesus' words to them and rather than hearing the Truth in His words, they turned on Him and tried to "catch" him in His own words. They wanted to use Jesus' own words against Him so they could turn the focus off themselves and onto His faults, thus justifying their own sin. How is this similar to the way an addict or "victim" may react and manipulate those around them?

Dealing with questions designed to malign us or "trip us up" can be frustrating and extremely painful. Yet, Jesus willingly engaged those who would oppose Him, choosing to state the Truth regardless of the consequences to His own life. Of course Jesus had the benefit of knowing He was sinless and is the Word of God. How can imperfect people like us stand firm like Jesus in the truth even when we know we have sin in our own lives?

Jesus did not allow others to manipulate Him . . . AT ALL. He was and is strong and truthful and wise. This should encourage us to seek His wisdom so that we too can answer the "Pharisees" in our lives. We must seek to spend time in the Word of God so that we can have that wisdom at our disposal at all times and we must be sure to have the Holy Spirit living inside us so that He can direct our words and guide our actions. Have you allowed Jesus to give you His Holy Spirit by accepting His gift of salvation? If not, standing in the truth will be extremely difficult if not impossible. We must know the Truth to share the Truth. James 1:5

5. How can we effectively deal with addictive personalities and victim mentalities while maintaining a biblical perspective and a Christ-like manner?

Look at the life of Christ, He was not considered weak, vulnerable or cowardly. Even when taken to the cross, it was by His choice and design. If we are to be Christ-like or imitate Christ, should our characteristics not be the same?

Read the following scripture and list out the characteristics Jesus displays in each instance:

John 5:1-15

John 8:1-11

John 12:44-50

John 8:34-38

Luke 13:31-35

Luke 5:12-13

Jesus healed many from physical, mental and spiritual ailments when on Earth and continues to do so today, but in order to be unbound from the slavery in which sin oppresses us He calls us to act. When Jesus forgave the adulterous woman (John 8:1-11), he told her to go and leave her life of sin. He didn't forgive her then allow her to return to that life of sinfulness. And when he healed the lame man (John 5:1-15), Jesus told the man to stop sinning, not to go about his regular habits.

Even as we engage in sin, Jesus is desperate to save us and bring us to Himself (John 12:44-50 and Luke 13:31-35). Jesus is always willing to clean us and desires a life of freedom for us (John 8:34-38 and Luke 5:12-13).

Christ IS love and we are called to love as He loves, but He did not condone sin or enable others to engage freely in it. Instead, in love, He called out sin, healed through forgiveness and then called the person to act on that gift by eliminating sin from their life, knowing the act of obedience would bring them to a life of freedom. He corrects us in love without compromising the Truth.

While Jesus is loving and forgiving and commands us to be the same, He did not act in cowardice or weakness. Instead He spoke and acted in authority—the authority given Him by God the Father. He doesn't condemn, but gives a choice—to obey and act in love or to continue in sin and be a slave to it.

In order to minister to or engage in a relationship with an addictive personality or anyone actively involved in a sinful lifestyle, your connection with Christ must be strong. You must walk closely and spend time with Him daily in the Word to be able to point others to Christ. We are called to be Christ-like, but we are not Christ, so we must always point others to Him. By maintaining a steady boundary and responding to such personalities with scripture references and advice that points them to biblical teaching, we are encouraging the person to develop their own relationship with Jesus and not to rely on people to fill their needs.

6. Carol quotes Franklin's poem about God weaving a tapestry of our lives and turning it into a beautiful work of art. Within that tapestry there are beautiful threads of joy as well as threads we may see as ugly or flawed. God uses them all to create His masterpiece. Left in our own hands, we would make a mess of the tapestry, not having the skill or vision necessary to see the final masterpiece, but when we place those threads in the hands of the Master Weaver, He creates something magnificent and meaningful. The flawed threads we may attempt to remove, the Master Weaver may use to make the entire work of art stronger, more brilliant and more interesting. The dark makes the light stand out more brilliantly.

What threads have you been trying to remove instead of giving them to the Master Weaver?

We may use many methods to attempt thread removal or to conceal the offending thread, which may result in more "ugly threads" or "snags" within our tapestry to deal with. For example, when we don't turn to Christ for our "fix", we may turn to something or someone else that is damaging. What "snags" have you developed as a result of trying to remove those threads?

Only in the hands of the Weaver can those "bad threads" be used for good purposes. God is the only one who can weave flawed threads into a work of art. We won't see the full beauty of our tapestry until we see it in the light of Heaven.

*If you or someone you know is struggling with this issue please seek professional help. Below are some available resources provided by the author for those struggling with sexual addiction or in a relationship with someone who is.

BOOKS

1. <u>Contrary to Love</u> by Patrick Carnes Ph.D
2. <u>Women Who Love Sex Addicts,</u> by Douglas Weiss
3. <u>False Intimacy,</u> by Harry W. Schaumburg
4. <u>The Final Freedom, by Douglas Weiss</u>
5. <u>Faithful and True,</u> By Mark Laaser
6. <u>Shattered Vows,</u> By Debra Laaser
7. <u>Seven Desires of Every Heart,</u> by Mark and Debra Laaser

ORGANIZATIONS

www.sexaddict.com Dr Weiss

www.sexualrecovery.com

www.celebraterecovery.vom

www.newlifepartners.org (for wives).

www.faithfulandtrueministries.com (Dr Laaser)

www.bethesdaworkshops.org (for addicts and spouses)

www.sexhelp.com (Dr Carnes)

www.purewarrior.org

www.Purelifealliance.org

CHOOSING COURAGE

Often when I think about the details of my past, it seems as if it is some story I've heard or something that happened to someone else. Even sadder to me is the sneaking suspicion that my story is not uncommon at all.

I was raised in a home that resembled a war zone. Peace was a foreign concept to me and fear was the order of the day. My parents were such interesting people. Dad was a raging but highly functioning alcoholic and a dominating control freak. Mom was a perpetual victim and habitual liar. How easily they got trapped in this cycle. Dad would be abusive and throw rage-fests to control us. Mom would play victim, often embellishing situations to friends and coworkers to get the attention she so desperately craved. Oh how they hated each other. I honestly have no memories of them being loving towards each other, or really being anything but enemies under the same roof. For seventeen years, this was the cycle. To be perfectly frank, they never should have gotten married. They got married each thinking it would solve their individual problems. Instead, they just combined problems that grew larger with each passing year. They each had their affairs, one of which finally ended their marriage. I know divorce is bad and it affects people their whole lives, but I have to be honest when I say, in situations like ours, when violence and turmoil are all there is, it is necessary. The day my father moved out was one of the happiest days of my life. Peace at last, so I thought. Unfortunately the peace was short-lived.

Mom soon started dating and verbalized her thoughts of us as "dead weight" that would ruin her chances of finding another man. Yet, despite dragging us along, she did get remarried. He is a nice enough man, but my mother couldn't stop herself from taking her fears out on us. She still thought that we would ruin everything for her. I lasted six months there, then moved in with my Dad. After all, he had really changed. It wasn't us who had made him so angry, it was Mom. It was my Mom who drove him crazy. It wasn't us, right? I could not have been more wrong.

The next three years were the darkest years of my life. My Dad's anger had been brewing for quite some time. So had his hatred for women and it didn't help that I look a lot like my mother. His drinking made it worse, as alcohol often does. With his "Jekyll and Hyde" personality, he would switch from being loving, fun and caring to dark, angry and violent. Life got hard. All of a sudden, I became responsible for all the work to be done in the house. Everything was inspected behind me. Anything slightly off would bring a drill sergeant style berating. This almost always involved yelling curses to and about me about three inches from my face. It was always right in my face with a bowing up and clenched fists, as if to nonverbally threaten that a beating could be next. Eventually I starting wishing he would beat me. At least then the police could hold him while I escaped. Now, of course, I am grateful he did not. I became a real life Cinderella, only I knew Prince charming was a lie. After all, I had watched my dad date. He was Mr. Perfect, sensitive, caring, funny, charming, and gentlemanly. That side was always short-lived. Then he would stop playing the role and turn into the controlling, manipulative, angry, violent man that he is at his core. He alienated me from friends and family as much as he could. I had to play my role of submissive, perfect daughter to gain a shred of freedom.

Pretty soon, based on the drunken ramblings spewing out of my dad's mouth, I could tell my life was possibly in jeopardy. I had no courage to get out and wondered how long I had left before he did something irreversible. The insanity in the house had gone through the roof. I knew my life was no longer of any value to my dad. At some point, in the constant rage, I ceased to be a person. I didn't know what to do or where to turn, so I cried out to God. I went to church until high school and I believed God existed, but I was very scared of Him. All my life I'd heard Him called my Heavenly Father and with the earthly example being all I knew, I preferred to stay off His radar. But here I was, trapped, with nowhere else to turn. The more the extremes grew, the more I pleaded for help, often wondering if He heard me or if He even cared. But, in my darkest times during this part of my life, when I was most worried, I would go outside and look up and see a rainbow. I knew a rainbow was the sign of God's covenant not to destroy the earth again by water. I felt He was telling me, "I will not let you be destroyed here. I will get you out of this."

I look back now and I see God's hand at work in so many details I didn't see then. God provided a coworker who was moving out of the country who sold me a car and everything in her apartment for beyond dirt cheap. I stored it in a self-storage unit for a few months. I asked the storage place not to send the rent notice, but they did every month. God was protecting me and the days it came proved to be the only days I got the mail rather than my Dad. God provided an apartment. Someone called my work saying they were returning a call about an apartment they had for rent. It was very affordable and my co-worker told her to hold it for me. So I found myself leaving one Friday night to sign a lease on an apartment into which I had no earthly idea how or when I was going to move.

I had it in the back of my head that the next time my dad travelled out of town for work, I would pack up and leave. Those plans changed very quickly. Sunday afternoon brought one of the worst rages I had ever experienced, triggered by my asking for help opening the door. It started with the normal yelling and cussing me out. It progressed to the expected attempt to convince me of what a worthless waste of space I was. Then it turned scary. I'll never forget his words. He started telling me how he had seen changes in me he didn't like. He made reference to my siblings, with whom he had no relationship at that time, going through the same changes. Then he looked me straight in the eyes and told me that if I was going down that same path to let him know and he would get his gun and send me straight to hell. I have never seen such evil hatred in someone's face before as I saw in his. This was not something I took lightly. He had very recently acquired a handgun and had rambled on about committing suicide and not going to jail. For quite a few months I had suspected he was planning to kill me and then himself. And there it was, out on the table. My suspicions had been confirmed. That night, after my Dad passed out, with my mind racing, I quietly packed as much as I could hide in my closet. The next morning he woke me up before going to work. As usual Dr. Jekyll was back being nice. I waited thirty minutes, called my friend's mother who had agreed to help me move, and I left. I thank God for the strength to get out that day. I shudder to think what could have happened if I had stayed. Through the years as I've looked back on this, there has never been a doubt in my mind Who got me out, even though He knew I would spend the next ten years in rebellion against Him.

Coming out of a situation like that had left me in shock. I couldn't even process it for a while. But as the shock subsided, my anger began to emerge and grow. Unfortunately, that anger brought along its cousins bitterness and distrust. I can look back now and honestly say I've lived most of my adult life "on guard", waiting for the bottom to drop out. I never wanted to admit it out loud, but I looked around at other people and their families and wondered, "Why? Why was this my life? Why did I have these parents?" I really did not think I had a right to ask. I mean God had gotten me out of a horrific situation. I didn't want to be ungrateful and start questioning Him. Besides, in my mind, it was easier to stay off the radar if I kept silent. But regardless of how stealthy I tried to remain, God never stopped pursuing me.

In my late twenties, God brought into my life a witness for true faith in Him. Not by her words alone, but by how she lived. I saw for the first time someone who lived for Christ and not herself. You see, my whole life, I had been preached at; told to fear God; taught God's anger; and definitely told many times that Hell was where I was going. And maybe, just maybe, if I played my cards just right, followed the rules, stayed away from bad things and bad people, and oh yeah, walked the aisle to accept Christ and get baptized, then MAYBE God wouldn't strike me down. I had been beaten over the head so many times with the Bible that, by this point, I had a permanent lump. But THIS woman, she did things I hadn't seen before. She would use scripture to correct herself rather than using it to judge others! Instead of shunning contact with those who acted in ways against her beliefs, she found ways to engage them and participate, all the while keeping herself blameless. She provided a physical example of walking in righteousness without being self-righteous. I watched for three years as she faced some of life's most difficult trials and never did she falter in her faith. She continued to praise God even during her most painful times. For the first time, I was seeing a faith that I wanted for myself.

All these things were whirling in my mind. I felt like God was calling me, but I was so desperately afraid of Him that I ran. I tried to hide from Him. I laughed out loud the first time I read Psalm 139, not because it is funny, but it was an "aha" moment. It starts by saying how God knows us inside and out, how He made us. Then verse 7 got me. David says, "Where can I go to escape Your Spirit? Where can I flee from Your presence?" It goes on to list many places that are not hiding places from God. Two things struck me. One, I can't go anywhere in God's creation to escape Him. Two, I'm not the only one who's tried. Thankfully, God in His love, did not allow me to hide. At 30 I gave my life to Christ. I didn't repeat the words of the prayer I'd said in my youth. I didn't follow a formula or have to "do" anything. I simply prayed in my bed one night and confessed to God I couldn't live without Him and I was tired of trying to go it on my own. I poured out my need for Him. I was struck when I read the story of Hagar fleeing from Sarah. Hagar was stranded in the desert with Ishmael. She was without water, without food, without hope. God, in His love, saw her and rescued her and her son. Oh how that story revived in me the memory of God seeing me and rescuing me.

As I started to grow in my faith, some things started bothering me. I had to deal differently with my Dad, who I still regarded as this huge monster and who I still had a fear would one day put a bullet in my head. I was convicted of how much I've been forgiven, yet at the same time, I was convicted of how much I refuse to forgive. There are many people in my life that I need to let go and forgive, but my father was the biggest. I wrestled with God over this. On the one hand, I wanted so badly to forgive as I had been forgiven. On the other hand, I wanted to hold on to the past with an iron fist. That has always been my safety net, to be on the look-out for trouble with anyone, especially my Dad. That little voice in my heart would say, "Give it to Me." The proud voice in my head would refuse. I really did not want to let go of the wrong that had been done to me. But I knew what I was really saying to God was that I thought I knew better how to handle this than He does. I kept thinking that my dad doesn't deserve to be forgiven, then the real question came up; do I? The truth is that I don't deserve to be forgiven at all. Yet, that's exactly what Christ has given me: true forgiveness and a clean slate. How dare I not forgive my Dad. How? I had no idea, but like most things in my life I have no clue how to handle, I prayed for God to do it for me. I have to be honest; forgiveness is not a once and done action. It is an ongoing process. At times it is really tough and at times it is really easy. It is also a very liberating process. I did not realize it would free me. I had been carrying around so many chains for so long. Anger, hatred, fear and bitterness are so heavy. I finally have a freedom like I've never known before.

My life with Christ is an ongoing process, as well. He peels away the layers one by one to reveal a better, newer me, releasing me from the chains that steal joy and freedom. My very desires have changed. A heart that delights in giving has overthrown the selfishness that once reigned. Where bitter words lived, only clean language now flows. Instead of trying to stay off God's radar, I now revel in attending and serving in church and seek out opportunities to grow in my faith at every turn. Not only have I experienced freedom through forgiveness, but I have learned I am completely free to be who God created me to be because of Who He is and what He has done for me.

CHOOSING COURAGE STUDY QUESTIONS

1. What type of parental role models did you have growing up?

How, if at all, did this influence your opinion of God, the Father?

The writer's violent and negative experience with her own father set the stage for how she would view the Heavenly Father in her early years. Ultimately she saw God for who He is and was able to choose a life of freedom despite the experience with her earthly father.

Read 1 Kings 15:9-15.

King Asa goes down in history as a king who did what pleased the Lord, one whose heart was fully committed to the Lord all his life. But Asa came from a legacy of generations of corrupt and evil rulers, including a father who set up and worshipped idols and a grandmother who ran shrines full of prostitutes.

Read 2 Chronicles 15:1-8.

After hearing the word of God, what did Asa do? (v8)

After he gained courage from the word, he turned that courage into action. He not only chose a path different from that of his family and culture, he, as king, called the entire country to repentance. What do you think made the difference for Asa to choose God's way rather than the way of his upbringing?

2. Choosing God's way always takes courage. Many things can get in our way and try to convince us not to make that choice, be it our rough upbringing, some tough circumstances or our cultural environment. Ultimately it is our choice and ours alone. We can either succumb to the weight of our circumstances or we can choose to take God's path and take courage, knowing the battle is truly His.

Imagine the opposition Asa would have had as he chose God's way and acted on it. The writer certainly had plenty of "reasons" to continue in some sort of destructive lifestyle, but she chose to have courage, to hope in God. What will you choose?

Do you have any areas in your life where you are using the experiences of your past or your current circumstances as excuse to remain inactive? List and describe them here:

3. Even before the writer fully understood her need for God, God was providing for her needs, as He has a purpose for her life.

Look back at your life. Can you identify times when God clearly provided for your needs or protected you, even if you weren't seeking His help?

There are numerous examples of God providing for His people in the Bible. Look up the following verses and record what God provided in each instance:

Exodus 16:1-4	
1 Kings 19:3-8	
Daniel 6:16-22	
Acts 12:5-11	
Luke 19:1-9	
Luke 4:31-37	
Luke 8:43-48	
Genesis 21:14-20	

Take courage knowing that God is faithful to provide even when we don't know to ask. How much more will He provide for us when we follow Him closely? "And my God shall supply all your need according to His riches in glory by Christ Jesus." (Phil 4:19) With what do you need to trust God right now?

4. Take a moment to **read Psalm 139:1-16.** Note which verses stand out to you personally. Why?

Think about the one person you would say you are closest to on this earth. Isn't it amazing to realize that God knows you more deeply than they do. Not even you know yourself as well as the God who formed you. He knows what you are going to say before you even say it. Does this comfort you to know this or it is a bit unsettling?

Jeremiah 29:11 says, "For I know the plans I have for you;" declares the Lord, "plans to prosper you and not to harm you; plans to give you hope and a future."

It should be of great comfort to us to know that God not only knows us deeply, but has plans to do good with us and for us. So why, then, do we sometimes try to hide or run from God and His plans? What stands in our way to block our trust? Let's take a look at a man who went to great lengths to run from God's plans, to hide from the task God gave him. Turn to the book of Jonah in the Old Testament and read his story. (It is much shorter to read than you may think and certainly much shorter than the book could have been if Jonah had acted with a different attitude!).

Jonah literally fled from God. He ran to another city, hopped on a boat and went the opposite direction God had instructed him to go. How do we run and hide from God's direction? Is it wrapping ourselves up in work or other obligations, neglecting God's word or church attendance? In the margin, list the top 3 ways you typically "run" from God's direction or try to hide from what He's telling you to do.

God wanted to use Jonah for one of the most incredible revivals in history, but Jonah didn't like that plan. God could have found another prophet to fulfill His plan, but because of His love for Jonah, He wanted him to have that experience. What was the result of Jonah's attempt to outrun God?

While we may never be swallowed by a large fish, we will probably face other consequences to our disobedience and find out like Jonah, that we cannot outrun the God of the Universe. Can you think of an example from your life when you were running? What measures has God taken to bring you back into His will, so His plans for you can be completed?

It is silly for us to think that we can hide from the God who created not only us, but every hiding place there may be in the universe! Knowing His plans are for us to prosper, exactly why would we want to hide in the first place?

5. As the writer came to know Jesus' forgiveness at the age of 30, she also became aware of the need to show forgiveness toward others. But, just like Jonah said, "Lord it is better for me to die than to live," sometimes our hearts would rather die with the anger than be pushed to let go and forgive one who has hurt us deeply.

Jonah wanted to hold on to what Ninevah had done because if he truly forgives, then all that sin would be forgotten and they would somehow "get away with it." Our writer has struggled with similar feelings in that she wanted to hold tightly with a clenched fist the anger so as not to forget or condone their behavior. Somehow it feels like if we forgive we are excusing the behavior and so we hold fast, not willing to let ourselves be vulnerable enough to offer forgiveness and somehow be at risk to be hurt again. Do you have people in your life that require forgiveness?

Are you able to forgive or do you find yourself clenching your heart and holding on to the wrong done to you?

Jesus gives us clear instructions on how to treat others in light of our own salvation through His forgiveness. **Read the parable of the Unforgiving Debtor in Matthew 18: 21-35.** How much had the first servant been indebted to the Master?

The amount the first servant had been in debt amounts to millions of dollars in today's economy. How much did the 2nd servant owe the 1st?

That amount adds up to only a few dollars and yet he refused to forgive the man the debt even after being forgiven of a much greater debt. How did the 1st servant's Master react upon hearing of his lack of mercy?

What then did Jesus say about the Father regarding our forgiveness of others?

Unforgiveness and Christ cannot live in the same body—there will not be peace. The two cannot coexist in harmony. We are literally torturing ourselves by trying to have it both ways.

6. The writer encountered a friend who gave a living testimony to Christ's Spirit living inside her. This friend did not judge, but corrected herself. She did not beat the writer over the head with the Bible, but provided a real-life example of what walking with Jesus looks like. We have all heard the saying "actions speak louder than words." What are your actions saying to others?

Think of someone whose actions have spoken of Christ to you. What did they do that made you take notice? What was different?

Read 2 Timothy 3:16-17(NIV).

Fill in the blanks:

"All scripture is _____-_____ and is useful for _____,
_____,
_____, and _____ ____ ____
_____,
So that the man of God may be thoroughly _____ for every
_____
_____."

What does this passage reveal about the nature and usefulness of scripture?

The writer's friend took this passage into practice, not only to provide wisdom and instruction to others, but to make sure she was "thoroughly equipped for every good work" herself.

Turn to Matthew 5:14-16 and read it silently to yourself.

Write that passage out right here.

Now, read it again, but out loud this time. Really chew on the words, what this message from Jesus is really expressing.

The light that burns inside a Christian is not their own, but the gift of light provided by the Holy Spirit through Jesus Christ our Lord and Savior. List some ways you can let the light of Christ shine openly in your life for the benefit of man, and the glory of God.

The Light we are referencing is only given when someone accepts Christ into their life. It is not obtainable without Him. We are the light of the world only as much as Jesus is the light of our lives. The most courageous thing you can ever do is to accept that Gift of Light into your life. If you have not already accepted this most precious Gift, please take the time now to pray and ask God to open your heart to Him. He is ready to hear from you and so very willing to forgive you and graft you into His family though His grace.

DAVID AND GOLIATH—

A 'What now?' from Kathy and Valerie

Wrestling with God. That is a term of which we now have some understanding. In Genesis 32 the story of Jacob wrestling with God is told. While his was an actual physical wrestling and ours was more a spiritual emotional wrestling, we can still say entering the ring with God is an exhausting fight you inevitably can never win. You either end up submitting to Him or you continue exiting the ring feeling exhausted and unsatisfied. We know because it took each of us a few rounds of partially submitting until we finally gave in and completely submitted to what it was God wanted us to do.

It was made very clear to us that God doesn't always ask us to do things that we are comfortable doing. Sometimes we have to step out of that boat onto unknown and uncomfortable water. What He has taught us through that; however, is that if we keep our focus on Him and not the water, then the water can never drown us. He will draw us closer to Him and in Him is where our strength lies.

So what now?

You have read some amazing stories and hopefully delved deep into scripture. Are you ready and are you willing to share your story of God's work in your life? There were many excuses that easily could have stopped us from sharing ours. If we had submitted to the weight of these excuses instead of to our God, we very easily could have avoided this book all together. As you read through our lists of excuses not to share and reason to share our stories, add your own excuses and reasons and really ask yourself which list will prevail.

Excuses, excuses . . .

1. My story is not dramatic/personal/important/tragic enough to help anyone.
2. **I** am not important enough.
3. It is embarrassing to me and possibly hurtful to others.
4. I am not a good speaker/writer

5. I may cry in front of others or allow others to see my vulnerability. I just don't do that.
6. People will know for sure that I don't have it all together. If they don't already, they will think less of me. I don't want to be seen as weak.
7. I will always wonder what people are REALLY thinking of me.
8. I don't want people to think that **I** think that I am something special OR that I am unloading on them.
9. I am not thin/beautiful/healthy as someone who has come through this SHOULD be—it won't encourage and may even DIScourage someone from stopping similar behavior if they think they will end up like me. I have no right to share this.
10. I will be forever judged, scrutinized for weight/eating habits/mental health/what I say once people know this. I will be tainted.
11. I don't want people to feel compelled to give compliments. They don't seem real when people attempt to "fix" my attitude with them.
12. I don't want to be identified with this as if it is STILL me. It's really like a different person I am discussing.
13. People will watch and wait to see if I mess up or don't uphold a standard they think I should.
14. My salvation may be questioned.
15. I may be tempted to fall back into old sinful habits.
16. The memories, faces and emotions will take over my thought life.
17. I just don't have the time and don't want to focus what time I do have on a past I have tried to forget.

And the big one:

18. Speaking of it will give it LIFE and POWER and the battle will intensify.

David and Goliath:

So, there it is: our innermost fears, our internal battles. There IS of course another side. Ultimately, we didn't let this bundle of fear and worldly rationale win. There is a shorter list that actually has greater power than those Goliath size excuses because it is God's list of why we SHOULD share the story of His glory in our lives. If the two lists were folded into little paper soldiers, one would be like David and one like Goliath. And just as David took down Goliath because He trusted God to win, our little David list struck the Goliath one and it tumbled. So . . . take a look at the David sized list God used to conquer that Goliath sized one . . . .

1. I am being CONVICTED to do so—and have been for a while.
2. Maybe, just maybe, it'll help someone else.
3. It could help encourage deeper fellowship/friendships centered in Christ.
4. It could help others understand me—where I have been—why I love God and hate lies, flattery, pretense and masks.
5. Help me to be the what-you-see-is-what-you-get person God wants me to be.

6. Remind myself of what God has done for me.
7. I will have the opportunity to allow God to turn a bad situation around and use it for His good.
8. I will lean on God for courage and strength to do this.
9. I will be freed from a life I have tried to keep secret.

And the big one:

10. **It will glorify God!!!**

Half as long, twice as strong.

Will you share your story of God's work in your life with someone?

While truly our stories are not about us, they are about God, no one else can tell the story God gave you to tell like you can. So be enCouraged—your story is the best witnessing tool god has given you.

Our Savior carries many names and is worthy of all.

JEHOVAH AZAR = The Lord my <u>Helper</u> (Ps. 30:10)
JEHOVAH AMAN = The <u>Faithful</u> Lord (Is. 49:7)
JEHOVAH GAAL = The Lord thy <u>Redeemer</u> (Is 49:26)
JEHOVAH-JIREH = The Lord will <u>Provide</u>. (Gen. 22:14)
JEHOVAH-M'KADDESH = The Lord Who <u>Sanctifies</u> (Lev. 20:8)
JEHOVAH-RAPHE = The Lord Who <u>Heals</u> (Ex. 15:22-2)
JEHOVAH-TSIDKENU = The Lord Our <u>Righteousness</u>
JEHOVAH TSUR = The Lord my <u>Strength</u> (Ps. 144:1)
JEHOVAH SHALOM = The Lord our <u>Peace</u>

Who is He to you?

Will you share Him?

Sincerely in His love,

Kathy Di Sarli and Valerie Crawford

The gift of salvation:

The gift of salvation is just that—a GIFT. If you have never asked Jesus to be Lord of your life and are now realizing your need for Him, please take a moment to pray. It is very simple. God loves you, He sent His Son to die for your sins so you could spend eternity in Heaven with Him. It is as easy as ABC—the only requirements are that you:

1. **A**dmit that you are a sinner in need of God's grace and salvation because otherwise it is impossible for you to get to heaven. (*For all have sinned and fall short of the glory of God.* Romans 3:23 and *The wages of sin is death.* Romans 6:23)

2. **B**elieve that Jesus is God's Son, that He died on a cross for your sins and then rose again on the 3rd day, resurrected into new life, AND that this gift is available to you through His sacrifice. (*For Christ died for sins once for all, the righteous for the unrighteous, to bring you to God. He was put to death in the body but made alive by the Spirit.* 1 Peter 3:18)

3. **C**onfess Jesus as your Lord and savior, asking Him to live in your heart and be ruler of your life. (*That if you confess with your mouth, "Jesus is Lord," and believe in your heart that God raised Him from the dead, you will be saved. For it is with your heart that you believe and are justified, and it is with your mouth that you confess and are saved."* Romans 10:9-10.)

It doesn't take a fancy, wordy prayer or formal proclamation: sometimes it is just a desperate plea from your heart begging God to take over and accepting the love of Christ into your life. It is the single most important, powerful and life-changing thing you can do and all you have to do is accept the gift—it is readily available and the price has already been paid.

HELPFUL HINTS FOR THE LEADERS

Introduction Week: Welcome in the women cheerfully, making sure to greet newcomers especially. A good and simple ice breaker for each week is to have each woman state her name and answer a silly question about herself. Try something like "What's your favorite ice cream". This first week it may be good to ask the women why they chose to join this Bible study.

After welcoming all the ladies in, introduce the book. Make sure to point out that each story will be unique, authored by a different woman, yet relatable to every woman in some way. Of course, each woman in your group is different in personality, yet relatable to one another in some way. Encourage them to read one story each week rather than reading through all the stories in one sitting. Remind them that doing the study questions will allow them to get them most out of each week's lesson.

We found that a good icebreaker game that worked well in introducing the idea of relating with other women was as follows:

Pair the women up in groups of two. Try to mix up the groups by combining women of different ages or personalities. Pass out an index card to each group. Give them 5-10 minutes to talk and get to know each other. In that time they must find at least 5 things that they have in common with each other. Examples would be things like being from the same town, having common hobbies, favorite foods or colors, etc... When they are finished have each group share what they discovered.

Talk about how many weeks it will take to complete this study and what day and time you will be meeting. Make sure they know if there will be any weeks that you have to skip or reschedule due to holidays, etc. Pass around an information sheet asking for email addresses and phone numbers. We found that a weekly email recap was a great way to stay in touch with all the members of the group including the ones that will have to miss sometimes. Just simply recap some of the main points you discussed, any prayer or praise reports that are turned in, and provide a reminder as to which story you will be going over at the next meeting. This really helps keep motivation and encouragement going in the group.

There is no telling where each story will take you as far as discussion. It has been different in each group we have facilitated. So be open but also be prepared to talk if discussion doesn't come naturally at the beginning of this study. By the end, everyone will feel much more comfortable in sharing.

Be mindful of the time each week so that women who have to leave at a certain time don't feel as though they are missing out.

Have fun! Women love to laugh!

We would love to hear how it goes!

Story #1 Pigpens Aren't Just for Prodigal Sons

Silly question of the week: If you could ask one Bible character one question, what would it be?

The discussion here can go in a few directions. You may have women dealing with prodigal children or you may have women who are trying to get through their own guilt of being the prodigal and the feelings that they are fighting because of it. Either way question #3 dealing with serving 2 masters is a great place to go. Many parents make what they are going through with their prodigals their master unintentionally. While former prodigals may need to hear that feelings of failure or unworthiness can master us instead of the forgiveness and freedom that comes with Christ as our master.

If you have young mothers, this is a great opportunity to discuss the importance of training a child in the ways they should go. Discuss the importance of the parents' role in teaching Christian behavior vs. just trusting the church to do it.

Take a moment to discuss the challenge given in question 4. You may even want to give them a few minutes to write something during your time together.

Make sure that the women understand that struggling with the flesh is something we all deal with. Even the most upright Christian woman they can think of struggles with her fleshly desires. There is not something wrong with them because they struggle with the flesh; however, it is their responsibility to learn how to battle their flesh in a Godly way resulting in victory.

A main point to look for: God's grace is for us all. It completely frees us to be able to used by Him no matter how far we have drifted. There is Hope!

Story # 2 Just Keep Swimming

Silly question of the week: Where is the craziest place you have ever gone swimming?

A good discussion question based on question #1 is comparing the world's view of a full life to God's view of the abundant life.

Be careful not to assume everyone in the group knows the Bible stories to which we refer in the study questions. You may want/need to briefly recap the story of Job before attempting to discuss.

Going over the athlete training chart as a group may help group members understand the importance of spiritual 'exercise' and help clarify any questions they may have. Remind them that running the race next to people who continually encourage and inspire them to race their best is important. We can all get caught up in defeat if we do not strategically place ourselves on a team that is focused on the goal and 'in it to win it'.

Story #3 Trust and Obey

Silly question of the week: What was your favorite childhood game?

This story is a good place to allow group members who are comfortable to share their salvation experiences with one another. It might be good to break into smaller groups to allow for adequate time for sharing. You may want to place any members who have questions about their salvation in your own group.

Question 3 is great for discussion. Be sure that everyone gets an opportunity to respond. This may lead into some great 'side' discussions. If you know your group well enough, you may be able to do the following activity:
Give each person an index card with their name on it. Pass the cards around the group and have the other women write one good thing they see that woman passing down to the next generation.

Even if the Bible stories are very familiar to some of the women, encourage them to reread the stories anyway and emphasize how even as adults, we learn and grow and see new things each time we read God's Word.

The story of Hannah can be very influential if your group is full of young mothers. Hang out there and get the mothers to really feel what it must have been like to be Hannah. The influence we have as Christian women and mothers can be phenomenal. Let us all spend time with the Lord so that influence is for the good of the Kingdom!

Story #4 Sufficient for the Day is its Own Trouble

Silly question of the week: What is your biggest phobia? (ie: spiders, snakes, etc)

All women seem to have worry down to an art form. This story can generate great discussions as you rarely will have a woman who hasn't experienced worry to an irrational level at some point! You can have fun with this one and laugh even as you get to the important point of letting go and trusting in God.

Encourage the women to share their daily miracle list and if they did not complete it, encourage them to do so and share the following week. You may want to make this an ongoing activity at the beginning of each session from here on out.

Peter is a great one to study and connect with. See if you all can imagine what must have been going through his head and play it out in your group.

A fun game you could try is a taste test where you provide something familiar to eat or drink but that is missing a key ingredient to make it taste good. Like lemonade without the sugar, unsweetened chocolate, cookies without eggs or without leavening, etc. Name what's missing and then perhaps have the 'real deal' available for snack. Be creative! Emphasize that tasting and seeing the Lord is good leaves us longing for Him when we attempt life without Him.

Story #5 Delighted

Silly question of the week: What is the best thing you have ever tasted?

A good discussion question could be "Why are we not satisfied with being our best, rather than the best?" Take the time to discuss the hazards of comparing ourselves to others rather than to God's standard.

Discuss again the importance of surrounding oneself with positive Christian influences. Remind them that not all relationships, even ones in church, are iron sharpening caliber.

Find out if anyone completed the dare for the week of sending a card to a friend.

The great romance chart in question 6 could open up some really great discussion. Allow yourselves to become immersed in what makes a great romance and really spend time understanding how a relationship with Christ fulfills even our deepest desires greater than any other relationship could.

Story #6 God Still Writes the Orders

Silly question of the week: Have you ever written a letter to a famous person? If so, who? If not, to whom would you write a letter if you could?

This story is a good place to discuss the basics of hearing from God, what folks are looking for in a church and what things/people are they making their 'captain'.

It could be a good opportunity to allow the women to share what they like about their own church and what drew them there.

A good group activity similar to the *Trust and Obey* activity, would be to have everyone write their name on an index card, pass it around the room and let each woman write a 'gift' she sees in that person on the card.
While question 5 may seem simple, it can be very eye opening, even for long time Christians, when discussed out loud. If time permits, initiate discussion on this topic.

You may want to end the session by emphasizing the benefit of memorizing the Word of God. See if anyone can recite Proverbs 3:5-6 from memory!

Story # 7 Why Not Me?

Silly question of the week: Name something from your bucket list.

This is a great opportunity to discuss the fact that the things that seem to happen TO us are really not about us. "It's not about me," is a good statement to remember!

Ask your group if anyone has any miraculous healing stories and how God was revealed through it.

For many, Paul's thorn makes him very relatable. It is good to remember that sometimes God has use for those 'thorns' in our lives. You may want to sit with this topic a while in your group. Mainly, allow the conversation to evolve naturally, just be conscious as the group facilitator of keeping folks 'on track' and encouraging 'talkers' to allow time for others to share.

As the facilitator you can help bring home the point that like with any currency account, you only get back what you put into a spiritual 'bank account'. You cannot draw on what you do not have.

A great way to end on a positive note after the heavy topics in this story is to allow the group members to spend time describing what they think heaven will look like. You may want to prepare ahead of time with some scripture references or excerpts from Alcorn's *Heaven* book to center the group on how God Himself describes it.

Story #8 Perfecting the Tapestry

Silly question of the week: What is the craziest fad you have ever bought into? (ie: bell bottoms, suspenders, big hair, etc)

This story tragically relates to so many women in this day and age. However, it is full of 'land mine' topics! Please gage the climate of your group and be mindful of the sensitivities of the women in your group. You will very likely have someone that is personally dealing with this issue to some degree. Ask the Lord to guide your discussion and listen to the prompting of the Holy Spirit. Be careful that the discussion does not devolve into a man or husband bashing session.

Having recent statistics available regarding sexual addiction, pornography, television programming, etc can be very helpful to open the eyes of the group. For example, in a Focus on the Family poll from 2003, 47% of all families said pornography is a problem in their home.

Make your questions very general – such as when discussing betrayal, talk about any betrayal, not just adultery. Most questions are able to relate in the broader sense, not simply to the SA, adulterous situations.

In question 3 when discussing cheap forgiveness, indicate that this is a big problem even for Christians. What are some of the indicators that you have offered cheap forgiveness? (Ie: not wanting to be in the same place as the other person, fake conversation, etc.)

Make sure the people in your group understand Christ's strength even while He was gentle, tender and forgiving. A good way to end this session may be by reading the Franklin poem at the beginning of the writer's story.

Story #9 Choosing Courage

Silly question of the week: If you could be one superhero, who would it be?

People generally enjoy discussing the types of role models they had growing up, but be sensitive to those who may not be comfortable sharing.

There can be no courage without fear. Fear is not the sin. Not acting appropriately because of the fear is where we fall. Discuss what courage really is. What does it look like in people the group says possess courage. Talk about some public figures who display uncommon courage.
Read aloud Matthew 5:14-16. Talk about how we are to be the light of the world.
Before adjourning, have the women make a plan of action. Discuss ways they will go out into the world and shine Christ's light.

If time permits and this is your last meeting, have the women take a few minutes to read David and Goliath at the end of the book. Spend a moment discussing the excuses and reasons the women relate to. Encourage them to make their own lists in the spaces provided at the sides of the page.

Before leaving that last time, be sure to come together and pray for one another, encouraging them in a deep relationship with Christ as they go out into the world.